THE ... ERNOR:
THEORY ... CTICE

Shane Bryans

and

David Wilson

First published in 1998
Second Edition in 2000
by Prison Service Journal

ISBN 0 9528413 1 2

Copies of this book are available from the publisher at:

Prison Service Journal
HMP Grendon
Grendon Underwood
Aylesbury
Bucks
HP18 0TL

Printed in Great Britain
Typeset and Printed at HMP Leyhill 2/2000 XLY H547

FOREWORD

BY THE DIRECTOR GENERAL OF THE PRISON SERVICE

The Prison Governor

In his 1991 report Sir Raymond Lygo described the Prison Service as 'the most complex and difficult management task I have ever encountered', this book offers an interesting insight into that management task in the unique role of the prison governor. The Prison Service is at a critically important stage in its development. Having regained confidence of ministers and the public, largely through the dramatic improvement in its primary task of keeping prisoners in custody and preventing their escape, the challenge is now to deliver the Prison Service's second objective which is to help to reduce crime by providing constructive regimes. This book sheds light on the performance of the role which is most critical in delivering that objective.

The second edition of the book contains new sections reflecting the greater understanding of the role of governor in terms of managerial competence and in terms of developments in the law. By explaining the multi-faceted nature of the governor's task the book should serve as a useful aide memoir for those who perform the role and an elucidation of Sir Raymond Lygo's often quoted remark to the wider audience.

MARTIN NAREY

PREFACE TO THE SECOND EDITION

The first edition of this book generated much discussion about the role, duties and competencies required of a governor. We were surprised at the overwhelming positive response it received and the large number of copies it sold (over 1,500 at the time of writing). The reviewers of the book were favourable and enthusiastic. The money generated from the sales of the book have supported the work of the Prison Service Journal.

In this second edition, the book has been completely updated and material added. We have incorporated changes suggested by reviewers and comments made by various readers. The book takes account of the outcome of the Prison Service Review and other structural changes in the Prison Service. More importantly, it includes the results of ongoing research about governing prisons and feedback from governors themselves about the job they do.

Chapter 1 has been updated to include a section on New Labour and its impact on the Prison Service. Chapter 2 on Governors has been expanded to include an exploration of the role of the governor, looking in particular at the leadership, interpreting, resourcing and representing roles which governors perform. A model job description for governors is now included together with excerpts from standing order 3A which sets out the governor's duties. Two new sections have been added to Chapter 2, one on the impact of the Prison Governors' Association and the second on area managers and the line management of governors. Chapter 3 now includes information about the MCI Senior Management Standards and a section on prison leadership and the leadership charter. It has also been expanded to include a discussion on public management competence, incident command competence and an exploration of prison management competence, using the results of recent research. The chapter on prison staff (chapter 4) has had additional sections added on subjects such as RESPOND and recent industrial relations developments. The section on prison officers explores more fully the exercise of discretion in the light of recent research. Chapter 7 now includes a new section on prisons and the law. Chapter 9 has been rewritten to incorporate the publication of the Prison Service Standards Manual and its likely impact. Details of the amended auditing arrangements and the audit programme have also been included. The Prison Service's Objectives and Principles which replaced the Vision, Goals and Values Statement are discussed together with the changes to the Key Performance Indicators and Key Performance Targets. An explanation of the new Strategic and Business Planning process has also been added to the chapter. The final chapter (10) on well governed prisons, now includes a discussion on the concept of the 'Healthy Prison' developed by HMCIP Sir David Ramsbotham. The section on the American perspective incorporates recent American Correctional Association work on 'current concepts in correctional leadership'. A new case study has also been added to the good governing in practice section.

Shane Bryans
HMYOI Aylesbury
January 2000

David Wilson
University of Central England

DEDICATION

This book is dedicated to:
Elizabeth, Jamie, Hannah and Jemma Bryans
and:
Anne Maguire, Hugo and Fleur Wilson

ACKNOWLEDGEMENTS

This book would not have been completed without the hard work of many people. In particular, we should like to thank: Catherine Fell and Chris Watts, of the Prison Service Library, for tracking down hundreds of references; Jane Liversidge for typing an endless number of drafts with such good humour and accuracy; Lynda Bedford for typing some early drafts.

The content of the book has been informed by many staff and prisoners with whom we have worked. We should particularly like to thank the following people whose inspiration and thoughts have had a direct impact on the content of this book: Andy Barclay; Andy Beck; Tony Borton; Kate Cawley; Ian Clark; John Dring; Peter Earnshaw; Michelle Jarman; Rachel Jones; Martin Jennings; Jerry Knight; Kevin Leggett; Martin Lomas; Paul McDowell; Dave McMillan; Stephen Pryor; Alistair Robertson; John Powls; David Scott and Claudia Sturt.

We would like to thank Peter Cameron for permission to reproduce his paintings in Chapter Six.

The second edition would not have been possible without the patience of Julia Carleton and Rosina Drummond who typed the amendments. Once again our thanks go to our families for putting up with our absence, whilst we were doing the research and writing the second edition. The continued support and enthusiasm of Carole Allen, Dave Roberts and Julia Couper were also much appreciated. For the amendments to the content of chapters 2 and 3 we are grateful for the work done by the role of the governor project team and, in particular, Chris Roden. Much of the content of the amendments has been informed by the Governors who kindly agreed to be interviewed as part of the project. The views and different approaches of colleagues who are governors in the central area have also done much to help crystallise the concept of 'good governing' contained in this book, so particular thanks are due to John Cann, Tony Ireson, Paul Manwaring, Clive Morris, Tim Newell, Clem Norman, Stephen Rimmer, David Watson and Edd Willetts.

We are once again very grateful to Peter Quinn who spent many hours reviewing the updated text and offering advice on further amendments, and to Dhao Wotherspoon for proof reading the second edition.

ABOUT THE AUTHORS

Shane Bryans is Governor of HM Young Offender Institution Aylesbury. He joined the Prison Service in 1986, having gained a law degree and a Masters degree in Criminology from the University of Cambridge. He has served in four prisons as a governor grade, completed two postings to Prison Service Headquarters and worked as Head of Management and Specialist Training at the Prison Service College. Whilst working in the Prison Service he has gained a Master of Business Administration degree from the Open University and a Master of Education degree from the University of Sheffield. In 1998 he was seconded to Cambridge University to take up a Cropwood Fellowship and in 1999 was elected a Fellow of the Royal Society of Arts. He has published numerous articles on the Prison Service and in 2000 edited a book 'Prisons and the Prisoner' (with Rachel Jones) about the work of the Prison Service.

David Wilson completed his PhD at the University of Cambridge in 1983. He joined the Prison Service in the same year as an Assistant Governor at HMP Wormwood Scrubs. He has worked as a governor grade at HMYOI Huntercombe/Finnamore Wood, HMPs Grendon and Woodhill, and in 1995 became the Head of Prison Officer and Operation Training for HM Prison Service. He resigned form the Prison Service in April 1997, and is now Course Director of the Diploma/Masters in Criminal Justice Policy and Practice at the University of Central England in Birmingham. He has published numerous articles on the criminal justice system and a recent book, 'What everyone should know about crime and punishment' (with John Ashton).

CONTENTS

INTRODUCTION

This book stems from a conviction that the work of prison staff in general, and prison governors in particular, is unique and distinct, and demands the development of special skills and qualities. Part of this distinctiveness is the nature of the prison itself. How is a prison organised? How can we distinguish a 'good' prison from one which is 'bad'? These might appear simple questions to answer, but would a politician, a prisoner, the 'man on the Clapham omnibus', or a prison governor all agree in their answers? If not, who would be right?

In choosing to analyse the work of the prison governor it is explicitly acknowledged that there are other key players who have important roles and responsibilities, not least prison officers themselves. However, whilst prison officers have long been the subject of research,[1] the prison governor has largely been ignored. Whilst monographs have appeared on the specific responsibilities a prison governor might have, or the nature of their training, outside of the United States, no single book has been devoted to their work or role.[2] Indeed whilst it is common for former policemen, or ex-soldiers - two groups of people with whom prison governors are often compared, and who have recently made an impact on how prisons are run[3] - to write autobiographies on their retirement, prison governors have rarely put pen to paper.[4]

1. JE THOMAS (1972) The English Prison Officer since 1850: A Study in Conflict, London: Routledge and Kegan Paul and H CRONIN (1967) The Screw Turns, London: John Long. (Cronin was the first General Secretary of the Prison Officers' Association, which was founded in 1941).

2. A key source in relation to aspects of the work of prison governors is the Prison Service Journal. See, in particular, J REYNOLDS, U SMARTT (1996) Prison Policy and Practice: selected papers from 35 years of the Prison Service Journal, HMP Leyhill: Prison Service Journal. In relation to the work of prison governors, or 'wardens' in the United States, see KN WRIGHT (1992) Effective Prison Leadership, Binghampton, NY: William Neil Publishing, and JJ DiIULIO (1987) Governing Prisons, New York; Collier MacMillan. The training of prison governors in England and Wales is discussed in PA WADDINGTON (1983) The Training of Prison Governors: Role, Ambiguity and Socialisation, Bromley, Croom Helm. There are very few modern books on the work of prison governors. However, of note see J KELLY (1967) When The Gates Shut, London: Longmans. (Kelly was governor of HMP Holloway from 1959 - 1966).

3. See in particular the reports made by Sir John Woodcock, a retired former Chief Inspector of Constabulary, and General Sir John Learmont. The relevance of their reports is described in Chapter 1. It should also be noted that the current Chief Inspector of Prisons and the first Prisons Ombudsman both have military backgrounds.

4. However, of relevance to this book, the autobiography of a former Director General of HM Prison Service is of great interest, and is perhaps the first true 'insider' account of the workings of the Prison Service. See D LEWIS (1997) Hidden Agendas: Politics, Law and Disorder, London: Hamish Hamilton.

We have also chosen to write about prison governors, as opposed to prison officers, and the range of specialists who work inside, for as Sykes observed from his American experiences, those who run prisons hold 'a grant of power without equal'.[5] As such, and as numerous criminologists have described, it is essential that prison governors who are invested with this power in law can be made accountable for their decisions and actions. This accountability can be viewed either as an internal process, involving various managerial or organisational checks and balances, or external to the Prison Service through the courts, the press or parliament, holding prison governors responsible for their actions and the actions of their staff. An effective prison governor also understands the subtleties and nuances of the special nature of prison culture. In short, the prison governor is often a conduit through which various interested parties, including prisoners themselves, make sense of what happens inside.

The importance of the prison governor in contemporary penology in England and Wales can be gauged by the comments of two former Directors General of HM Prison Service. The first, Chris Train, Director General 1983-1991, commented that 'the key manager in the Prison Service is the governing governor. The Department's policies are delivered by him and his staff in the establishment for which he is responsible'.[6] Similarly Derek Lewis, the only Director General ever to have been recruited into the Prison Service from a commercial background, described the importance of establishing good relations with his governors early in his tenure: 'the key group I had to get to know were the prison governors'.[7]

This book is intended for the informed reader. As such we have presumed a background knowledge of some aspects of life inside. However, we have also attempted to provide, in the opening chapter, a context through which to understand what comes later. We have kept footnotes and references to a minimum, although we accept that some references may be difficult for the average reader to obtain, given that they refer to internal Prison Service documents. Unfortunately this was sometimes unavoidable, but we again have attempted to keep these to a minimum, and have largely used materials - either through official reports, or the Prison Service Journal - which are in the public domain.

5. G SYKES (1958) The Society of Captives, Princeton NJ, University Press, p42.

6. CJ TRAIN 'Management Accountability in the Prison Service', in REYNOLDS and SMARTT (1996), op cit, p153.

7. LEWIS (1997), op cit, p23.

Finally, we have chosen to write about prison governors because we are, or once were, prison governors. As such we believe that our professional colleagues should no longer suffer being stereotyped as either the buffoons from 'Porridge' or other comedies, or as the sadists who seem to run prisons in the eyes of Hollywood. Whilst most careers suffer a similar fate at the hands of popular culture, the absence of any realistic voice challenging these stereotypes ultimately affects the very nature of the debate itself. This silence, perhaps a reflection of the secrecy which has traditionally dominated the Prison Service as a whole, has to be ended, and we hope that what follows will contribute to that process.

CHAPTER 1

A SHORT HISTORY OF IMPRISONMENT

The beginnings of the Prison Service 1877-1966

There is no one history of prisons and imprisonment and thus choosing any starting point is merely one way to begin a particular interpretation. However, 1877 seems as reasonable a place as any to start this short history for in that year, with the passing of the Prison Act, the foundations of a modern, centralised Prison Service were laid. In particular the control of all prisons came under a Prison Commission which introduced, amongst other changes, the appointment of all prison warders, paid for by central government; standard training, uniform and disciplinary procedures to which all staff were subjected. This starting point also reflects a theme of this book. Namely, we have chosen a date, and will choose others, which reflect key moments in the organisation and running of the Prison Service, as opposed to those which reflect changes in legislation or social policy.

The main philosophical consequence of the 1877 Act was the decline of the rehabilitative rhetoric and impulse that had dominated the preceding years. Instead of rehabilitation, deterrence and punishment were promoted as the basic principles of imprisonment. These principles are best symbolised in the appointment of Edmund Du Cane as the first chairman of the Prison Commission, a position he was to hold until 1895, and the 'separate system' of managing inmates. Du Cane ushered into prisons a regime which was rational and uniform throughout the country and which emphasised the need to comply with common, centralised standards on such matters as, for example, hygiene and cleanliness. All prisons were to conform to these standards and all prisoners were to be treated alike - there was no place for individuality in Du Cane's Prison Service. As Du Cane was to write, 'A sentence of penal servitude is ... applied on exactly the same system to every person subjected to it. The previous career and character of the prisoner makes no difference in the punishment to which he is subjected'.[1]

In many senses the 1877 Prison Act reflected the spirit of its age, and Du Cane was merely emphasising the same desires for systematic

1. EF DU CANE (1885) The Punishment and Prevention of Crime, London: MacMillan, p155.

uniformity in prison as were evident in other spheres of Victorian life. Yet in denying individuality it became practically very difficult to treat every prisoner as if they belonged to the same criminal stereotype so beloved by the Victorians. Should first offenders be treated in the same manner as career criminals? Should young offenders and women be kept apart from the main body of prisoners? Indeed as early as 1838 a separate juvenile prison had been set up at Parkhurst, and in 1853 Brixton had been established as a women's prison.

However, the major criticisms of Du Cane centred on the problems of short sentenced prisoners, and recidivism. In the 1890s the average duration of all prison sentences was 28 days and thus the majority of prisoners were serving very short periods of custody.[2] In common with our own time, putting people into custody was a costly business, and incarcerating large numbers for very short periods of time led inexorably to overcrowding. Similarly, in denying prisoners their individuality, and elevating punishment and deterrence as guiding principles, those who were released tended to re-offend very quickly and return to prison.

The disillusionment of many with the consequences of the 1877 Act, and with Du Cane's regime, resulted in a clamour for change which became enshrined in the Gladstone Report of 1895. The influence of the Gladstone Report should not be underestimated and, in effect, it re-invented rehabilitation, albeit for only certain categories of offenders. So first offenders, young offenders, women, children and alcoholics were to be recognised as falling outside of the traditional criminal stereotypes and thus accorded different treatment. Du Cane was replaced as Chairman of the Prison Commission by Sir Evelyn Ruggles-Brise, who served as Chairman until 1921 and who, by 1898 had, for the first time, defined the purpose of imprisonment as being for 'the humanisation of the individual'.[3] As such numerous changes to the standard prison regime were introduced, including an end to unproductive prison labour and the introduction of 'useful work'; the replacement of the separate system by association; the use of remission to control prison discipline; and the introduction into prison of specialists, such as psychologists. Inspectors, introduced by the 1877 Act, were made accountable to the Home Office, rather than the Prison Commission and

2. GF MUNCIE (1996) Prison Histories: Reform, Repression and Rehabilitation, in E McLAUGHLIN, J MUNCIE (eds) (1996) Controlling Crime, London: Sage Publications, p190.
3. Quoted in MUNCIE (1996), op cit, P190.

a system of borstals was to be introduced, aimed at the reform of young offenders.

Even in these five paragraphs several echoes of our current preoccupations should have become apparent. Should prisons be for punishment, or rehabilitation? Should all prisoners be treated alike, or dealt with on the basis of their individual needs? Do young people, and women have different demands which should be accommodated whilst they are incarcerated? These questions are sometimes characterised as being part of the 'aims' debate about prisons and it is also interesting to note that, in under 20 years, the fundamental philosophical basis of the work of the Prison Service altered almost completely. Yet, as has so often been the case, this new philosophy was merely grafted onto the old, confusing the message of what was to be done and by whom. This is no small matter, for the question of the philosophical basis of imprisonment is inextricably linked to the objective we pursue, as a society, when we choose to incarcerate. Is the Prison Service being asked to incapacitate, rehabilitate, punish, deter, or extract retribution? Worse still, is it being asked to do all of these things at the same time?

Ruggles-Brise, like Du Cane before him, was a product of his time, and thus whilst changes were being introduced into prison, society itself was moving just as dramatically, under the Liberal governments of Campbell-Bannerman and Asquith. The issue of women's suffrage, the introduction of old age pensions, and the founding of the Discharged Prisoners' Aid Societies in this period all give some indication of life outside the prison walls. More importantly it was at this time that the prison ceased to be viewed as either the best, or the only method for dealing with offenders, and was instead seen merely as one of a series of options. Indeed there was a growing scepticism about what prisons could do, partly prompted by politicians such as Winston Churchill, who was Home Secretary 1910-1911, and who famously declared that 'the mood and temper of the public in regard to the treatment of crime and criminals is one of the most unfailing tests of the civilisation of any country'.[4]

This scepticism heralded a major reduction in the numbers of those being incarcerated. Between 1908 and 1938 the prison population fell from 22,029 to 11,086, a fact made all the more remarkable given that the recorded crime rate increased by 100 per cent during the same period.[5]

4. Quoted in A RUTHERFORD (1984) Prisons and the Process of Justice: The Reductionist Challenge, London: Heinnemann, p126.

5. Ibid, p43; pp123-126.

Nonetheless, opposition to the use of imprisonment hardened after the First World War with the publication of the Webbs' *English Prisons under Local Government* and a companion volume, *English Prisons Today*, by Stephen Hobhouse and Fenner Brockway, who had been incarcerated as conscientious objectors.[6] In 1921 The Howard Association became the Howard League for Penal Reform and in 1922 Alexander Paterson was appointed to the Prison Commission. Paterson was to remain a Prison Commissioner until 1946 and his influence, particularly over the development of the borstal system, was immense. The decline in prison numbers, and the general scepticism about imprisonment meant that, between 1908 and 1938, 25 prisons were closed.[7]

From the end of the Second World War until 1970 the prison population increased at an annual rate of five per cent.[8] Despite a Labour government coming to power and ushering in an age of social reconstruction, the Criminal Justice Act of 1948 took a hard line on law and order, perhaps best symbolised by the introduction of detention centres. Fear of crime, especially committed by young people, and a general view that very little could be done to stop crime, led to a greater use of custody, and a corresponding increase in the numbers of staff employed. Inevitably, overcrowding became an issue and, by 1950, 12 per cent of the prison population were sharing cells.[9] By 1963 the Prison Commission had been dissolved, and responsibility for the administration of prisons passed on to the Prison Department within the Home Office, inevitably linking the work of prisons very directly with that of the politics of the Home Secretary.[10]

At the end of this period two events can be seen as indicative of the competing demands of what had gone before, and of what would come afterwards. In 1964, reflecting the reformative impulse of the Gladstone Committee which had wanted people to leave prison 'better women and men, both physically and morally, than when they came in', Parliament approved the Prison Rules, which organise the daily lives of staff and prisons, the first of which required that 'the training and treatment of convicted prisoners shall be to encourage and assist them

6. S and B WEBB (1922) English Prisons Under Local Government, London: Longman, Green and Co: S HOBHOUSE, AF BROCKWAY (eds) (1992) English Prisons Today, London: Longman, Green and Co.

7. RUTHERFORD (1984), op cit, P147.

8. Ibid, p52.

9. Ibid, p64.

10. Prison Commission Dissolution Order SI 1963/597.

to lead a good and useful life'.[11] This must have been ironic given how prisons had developed since 1945, and was certainly to be challenged by events that followed in the wake of the theft of £2.5m from the Glasgow to London mail train at Cheddington in Buckinghamshire in August 1963. 'The Great Train Robbery' as it become known, and in particular the incarceration and subsequent escapes of some of the gang, were fundamentally to alter how prisons worked.

Mountbatten to May and beyond, 1966-1986

Most of the Great Train Robbers received sentences of 30 years which, with remission, would mean that they would serve 20 years. At the time only the spy George Blake had a longer sentence. Crime is essentially a young man's business, and the problems associated with keeping this age group incarcerated for long periods of time, when all they can see in their future is being released as old men, is one of the any problems faced by the Prison Service. Escape is an attractive alternative, and was an option successfully pursued by Charles Wilson who escaped from HMP Birmingham in August 1964; by Ronald Biggs who escaped from HMP Wandsworth in July 1965; by George Blake from HMP Wormwood Scrubs in October 1966; and by Frank Mitchell from HMP Dartmoor in December 1966. So great was the media interest in prison escapes that one news programme ended by displaying a scorecard of escapes as if prisons were competing against each other.[12]

The Mountbatten Report was the government's response to these failures in prison security and it had a major impact on how the Prison Service was to develop over the next 30 years.[13] In essence the Mountbatten Report is famous within the Prison Service for what it did, and did not do. In relation to the former it led to the introduction of the rank of senior officer; dog sections; closed circuit television systems and other electronic devices. More importantly it introduced a security categorisation system for prisoners into A, B, C and D (see figure 1), and recommended that all category A prisoners should be held together in a specially constructed prison, to be built on the Isle of Wight and called Vectis. Vectis was never built, and instead the government accepted the advice of a sub-committee of the Advisory Council on the Penal System, chaired by Professor Leon Radzinowicz, to disperse rather than

11. Home Office (1964) The Prison Rules, 1964, London: HMSO.

12. Quoted in RUTHERFORD (1984), op cit, p77.

13. Report of the inquiry into Prison Escapes and Security (Mountbatten Report) (1966) Cmnd 3175, HMSO, London.

concentrate the category A prisoners.[14] By 1970 there were seven dispersal prisons - HMPs Albany, Gartree, Hull, Long Lartin, Parkhurst, Wakefield and Wormwood Scrubs - which had high staff-inmate ratios and which were extremely costly to run. Indeed by the Home Office's own estimates, implementing the Mountbatten Report resulted in a 40 per cent increase in staff numbers between 1966 and 1978.[15]

Figure 1 : Mountbatten Report Security Categories

Category	Definition
Category A*	Prisoners whose escape would be highly dangerous to the public or the police or to the security of the state
Category B	Prisoners for whom the very highest conditions of security are not necessary, but for whom escape must become very difficult.
Category C	Prisoners who cannot be trusted in open conditions, but who do not have the ability or resources to make a determined escape attempt.
Category D	Those who can be reasonably trusted to serve their sentences in open conditions.

*Category A now has three sub divisions: standard Category A; high risk Category A; and exceptional risk Category A

The dispersal prisons had problems almost from their inception. There were riots at HMPs Albany and Gartree in 1972, and a particularly damaging one at HMP Hull in 1976. There was a further riot at Gartree in 1978, and at the dispersal wing of HMP Wormwood Scrubs in 1979. The special interest group PROP (Preservation of the Rights of Prisoners) was formed in 1972 and organised a sit down demonstration in HMP Brixton in April of that year. Over the next few months there were 130 demonstrations by PROP in prisons up and down the country, culminating in a call for a prisoners' national strike in August 1972. Over 4,000 prisoners took part in 26 prisons, demanding the right to vote, to belong to a trade union, and to conjugal visits.[16]

This new mood of militancy can be gauged by the growing numbers of local disputes between management and the Prison Officers' Association (POA). Between 1972 and 1975 there was an average of five disputes per year; between 1976 and 1980 this average

14. There are numerous accounts of the Mountbatten / Radzinowicz debate, and whether 'concentration' is better than 'dispersal'. Of great interest is the account of Leo Abse MP who was a member of the sub-committee chaired by Radzinowicz, and who gives a direct insight into how the debate was influenced at the time. See L ABSE (1973) Private Member, London: McDonald, pp132-3.

15. RUTHERFORD (1984), op cit, p79.

16. Ibid, p79.

number had risen to 74 per year.[17] These disputes made running a prison a very difficult task indeed, made all the more complex by the fact that governors had no control of the 'daily detail' which allocated officers to work. Thus each prison effectively ran on overtime. In 1978 overtime accounted for 37 per cent of average gross earnings for officers and senior officers.[18] A governor who wanted to challenge this state of affairs would first have to learn the 'mystery' of the detail, and then be prepared to cope with any industrial action which might ensue.[19] This industrial action took the form of a 'work to rule', effectively suspending a willingness to work overtime, rendering a prison almost incapable of functioning. One prison governor, until recently an Assistant Director, described the result of this state of affairs thus 'the control of prisons had by the mid seventies, to a very large extent, passed into the hands of the Prison Officers' Association'.[20] In short there were perpetual disputes about staffing levels, pay and specialist allowances.

As a consequence, the May Committee was set up in 1978 to inquire into the state of the Prison Service. Its purpose was primarily to recommend on such questions as staffing, resources and management and its major impact was to prepare the ground for the managerial initiatives of the mid-1980s in relation to the 'three 'E's': economy, efficiency and effectiveness. However, the committee also advocated a view about the purpose of imprisonment, thus contributing to the 'aims debate', based on an idea of 'positive custody', as a revision of Prison Rule 1. This was promptly attacked by numerous academics as having no real meaning and two vehement critics, King and Morgan, responded by advocating their own views of 'humane containment'.[21] Whilst it would be fair to conclude that 'humane containment' has been more favourably received than 'positive custody', the debate was effectively lost as other priorities emerged with the election of a Conservative government in 1979.

The new government was elected on a 'law and order ticket' and a great deal of the new tone was set by the use of the 'short, sharp shock'

17. Ibid, p85.

18. Ibid, p96.

19. On joining HMP Wormwood Scrubs as a new assistant governor in 1983 one of the authors was physically excluded from entering the detail office. This was by no means an uncommon experience.

20. Arthur de Frisching quoted in RUTHERFORD (1984), op cit, p86. See too 'Who runs the prisons?' 1982 PL346.

21. RD KING and R MORGAN (1980) The Future of the Prison System, Farnborough: Gower.

in detention centres. Whilst this had not been mentioned in the party's election manifesto, it become almost a rallying cry to those who wanted to 'get tough' or at least 'do something'. The borstal system was replaced by youth custody in 1984 and the old problems of order and overcrowding continued to make their impact. Between 1946 and 1986 the prison population increased from 15,000 to 45,000 and overcrowding was especially acute in the old, Victorian local prisons such as HMP Bedford, HMP Gloucester and HMP Leicester. Nor had the issue of staffing and staff resources disappeared, especially when set against a background of significant increases. The staff-inmate ratio in 1986 had been one officer to every 2.6 prisoners whereas in 1946 it had been one officer to every seven.[22]

However during this period, building on the work of the May Committee, attempts were made to redefine the purpose of imprisonment by the Director General, Chris Train, using the device of Circular Instruction 55 of 1984.[23] Similarly a far-reaching race relations policy statement was published, and race relations liaison officers were introduced into each Prison Service establishment. Ian Dunbar, a Regional Director, contributed to the ongoing 'aims debate' with *'A Sense of Direction'*[24] and in particular in his use of the concept of 'dynamic security', based on the principles of individualism, relationship and activity. Likewise the Control Review Committee attempted to define positive aims for long-term prisoners in the dispersal estate.[25] Nonetheless, real change lay in the next period, although that could not have been achieved without the developments described above.

From 'Fresh Start' to the present day, 1987-2000

The last ten years have seen unparalleled changes in how the Prison Service operates and is managed, whilst at the same time persistent problems refuse to disappear. Criminologists will usually describe the inability of the Prison Service to resolve these issues as

22. RUTHERFORD (1984), op cit, p96.

23. A copy of C1 55/84 together with Train's rationale for its introduction, can be found in J REYNOLDS and U SMARTT (1996) Prison Policy and Practice: Prison Service Journal, pp152-159.

24. I DUNBAR (1985) A Sense of Direction, London: HMSO. Since 1981 five Circular Instructions on race relations have been issued. Of note C132/1986 requires that all prisons publicise an accountable race relations policy.

25. Home Office (1984) Managing the Long Term Prison System. The Report of the Control Review Committee, London: HMSO.

being at the heart of the system's perpetual 'crisis'.[26] This crisis, in particular, is seen as being centred on such issues as legitimacy - the way in which the exercise of power over prisoners is justified and accounted for - and the Prison Service's aims. Both issues are important and there were clear efforts to tackle them during this period through the introduction of internal accountability measures and by the publication of a 'Mission Statement'. Perhaps for prison staff this idea of crisis would be more closely related to the seemingly never-ending problems of a rising prison population, overcrowding and the need to maintain order.

To choose 1987 as a starting point for this section relates to the introduction of a package of proposals known as 'Fresh Start'. Yet the roots of 'Fresh Start' can be traced as far back as Circular Instruction 55/84 which, for the first time, attempted to organise the work of every Prison Service establishment around certain basic tasks (see Chapter 3). In other ways this search for roots should go further back into history, as 'Fresh Start' was a major initiative aimed at changing the fundamental institutional character of the Prison Service as a whole. Indeed, whilst it is only right to acknowledge the perennial problems of rising numbers and disorder - and the riots of 1990 were a clear, defining moment for the Prison Service - this was also a period which has been characterised by innovative, strategic thinking about what it is that the Prison Service should do, and how it should be done.

The acceptance and introduction of 'Fresh Start' saw the ending of prison officers' overtime, paid with their wage on a weekly basis, and its eventual replacement by a monthly salary based on a 39 hour working week. At the same time the grading structure of the Prison Service was rationalised with the abolition of the chief officer and assistant governor ranks, and their amalgamation into governors 5 and 4 (see figure 2). In theory this allowed an officer to be promoted 'through the ranks' to governor 1. Previously the vast majority of staff had set their sights on becoming 'chiefs', especially as the governor grade ranks were seen principally as the preserve of university graduates or retired senior forces personnel. This largely symbolic unification of the rank structure was partially undermined, in the eyes of some staff, by the introduction of an Accelerated Promotion Scheme (APS), but has become increasingly important as time has worn on, and

26. For issues related to the idea of 'crisis' and its limitations, see R SPARKS (1996) 'Prison, Punishment and Penalty' in E McLAUGHLIN and J MUNCIE (1996), op cit, pp197-247.

principal officers have been promoted to the governor grades. Finally, 'Fresh Start' rationalised the work of each prison into a series of 'functional blocks' such as residential, operations and inmate activities, and created 'model' management structures for each size of prison.

Figure 2: Grade Structure of HM Prison Service (Unified Operational Grades)

Pre Fresh Start	Current Grades
Governor 1	Governor 1
Governor 1	Governor 1
Governor 1	Governor 1
Governor 2	Governor 2
Governor 3	Governor 3
Governor 4	Governor 4
Assistant Governor	Governor 5
Assistant Governor T (under training)	
Chief Officer 1	
Chief Officer 2	
Principal Officer	Principal Officer
Senior Officer	Senior Officer
Prison Officer	Prison Officer
Prison Auxiliary	Operational Support Grade

All of this seems reasonable enough several years later, but at the time there was great debate and much controversy. The Prison Service is inherently conservative, and the issue of overtime, with the vast amounts of money it could generate, and the industrial muscle that could be wielded by threatening to 'work to rule', effectively withdrawing a willingness to work overtime, meant that the stakes were very high indeed. The guiding architect of 'Fresh Start' was Eric Caines, and some years later, in an interview in the Prison Service Journal, he described how negotiations had gone with the National Executive of the Prison Officers' Association. As Caines saw it, the Prison Service was effectively offering the POA a deal of 'terms and conditions of service in return for reasonable conditions for prisoners'. However, everything did not go as planned.

> 'The POA executive were in session on the Sunday morning, and I got a call in my office from David Evans, who is a wily old bird, and who gives the POA some respectability. He asked for some compromises and amendments to make things easier on two or three occasions in the course of that Sunday morning. I did make some compromises. However, I knew it

couldn't go on or the integrity of the package would be ruined. At around 12 the phone went again, and I knew I had to say no. That was it - the overtime ban, but I knew that we had good contingency plans ... we had a few difficult days ... but it did calm down. Largely I think because the more reasonable (local) POAs didn't like what was happening (and) exercised pressure on the NEC.'[27]

The importance of the introduction of 'Fresh Start' should not be underestimated. It could be argued that many of the benefits gained by its introduction have continued to pay dividends for the Prison Service. The power of the POA, which at the time had been all-consuming, never again seemed so great, and governors through the introduction of functional related management structures, and the SPAR system,[28] found mechanisms which allowed them to manage their prisons. Perhaps most significantly, the officers 'on the landings' could genuinely feel that, through application and effort they could move up a career ladder which would include the highest ranks in the Prison Service.

The late 1980s saw the growing emergence of an issue which was to dominate the larger philosophical debate about the purpose of imprisonment and its relation to the state: privatisation. In 1987 Douglas Hurd, at the time Home Secretary, was to declare that he saw no place for privatisation in the Prison Service of England and Wales.[29] Yet a little under a year later the Green Paper, 'Private Sector Involvement in the Remand System'[30] was published and led directly to the opening of the first prison contracted out to private management, The Wolds, near Hull in 1992.

27. D WILSON, Interview with Eric Caines, in REYNOLDS and SMARTT (1996), op cit, pp 172-178, quote on p176.

28. SPAR - Staff, Planning and Reporting - is a management system which accounts for the numbers of hours worked by officers, senior and principal officers. All governing grades were trained in this system as part of their 'Fresh Start' conversion training. The system has been refined, but is still in operation. Governor grades are not themselves subject to SPAR accounting, as they are 'all hours worked' grades.

29. For the origins and early development of privatisation in England and Wales, see S SHAW, A Short History of Privatisation, in J REYNOLDS and U SMARTT (1996), op cit, pp 168-172. The most scholarly account of privatisation is M RYAN and T WARD (1989) Privatisation and the Penal System, Milton Keynes: Open University Press. For a prison governor's view about privatisation see D SAUNDERS-WILSON, Privatisation and the Future of Imprisonment, Prison Service Journal, April 1986, pp7-9.

30. Home Office (1988) Private Sector Involvement in the Remand System, Green Paper, London HMSO.

The debate about privatisation is important as it evokes much wider moral issues which are at stake in the Prison Service. On the one hand, so the argument goes, the best prison is the one which provides the best conditions, whether that be public or private; on the other, it is simply wrong to delegate a responsibility of the state to a private contractor who in effect, makes money out of the misfortune of others, and who will benefit from ever greater numbers being incarcerated. These problems have been characterised as 'consequentialist' and 'intuitionist'. In all of this the consequentialists have been helped by the development of a managerial culture in the Prison Service, or 'managerialism' as it is sometimes described.

This emphasises the basic neutrality of prison staff in relation to moral questions, and concentrates instead on how good business practice can best be applied to make a prison more efficient. Effectively governing a prison is seen as involving more or less the same principles as managing a supermarket or a department store and thus can be justified the extension of the 'market testing' process to design, build and then manage prisons. As such the metamorphosis of the Prison Service in 1993 from a department of state within the Home Office to a free standing 'Next Steps' Agency, under a new Director General recruited from private industry, was seen as symptomatic of this new managerialism.[31]

However, the internal re-organisation of the Prison Service in September 1990 was perhaps more significant than the acquisition of Agency status. The report on which the re-organisation was based was prepared by external management consultants - PA Consultants - and concerned itself with efficiency savings, shortened and accountable line-management arrangements, the roles of specialists and the handling of information.[32] The report accepted that 'Fresh Start' had dealt with the work of establishments, and therefore concentrated on the regional and national levels of the Prison Service. It argued for 'flatter' management structures, and greater accountability - or supervision - of governors. It also argued for a 'tighter integration of

31. Brian Caffarey was head of the Agency Unit set up in March 1992 to guide the Prison Service through to Agency status. He wrote the benefits of the Agency in 'Agency Status' in Perspectives in Prisons: A Collection of Views on Prison Life and Running Prisons, A Supplement on the Work of the Prison Service, April 1991 - March 1992 (HMSO 1992), pp39-40. The Director General referred to is Derek Lewis, who before his appointment had never visited a prison. Lewis has written about his recruitment in LEWIS (1997), op cit, pp 1-15.

32. PA Consultancy Group: HM Prison Service - Review of Organisation and Locality above establishment level, August 1989.

policy and operations'.[33] Its principal recommendation was the abolition of the four regions of the Prison Service and their replacement by 15 area offices, later reduced to 12 with the addition of a Dispersals Directorate. Area managers, who would be senior to any of the governors in their area, would have operational responsibility for the area but not all the area managers would necessarily have an 'operational' background, and some would come from other parts of the Civil Service. This caused a certain amount of disquiet, and was attacked, for example by the Prison Governors' Association (PGA), as being 'irresponsible, given that area managers would be in command during riots or hostage situations'.[34]

However, whilst the managers are in the ascendancy, they have not had things all their own way. The 1988 Prison Service Mission Statement, for example, whilst hardly revolutionary or indeed as far-reaching as the comparable Scottish Prison Service statement, echoes the old Prison Rule 1 and is, at the very least, an optimistic declaration of what the Prison Service should do, at a time when 'humane containment' was as much as was felt possible. It deals implicitly with morality and provides a positive context in which prison staff must work:

> Her Majesty's Prison Service serves the public by keeping in custody those committed by the courts.
> Our duty is to look after them with humanity and help them lead law-abiding and useful lives in custody and after release.

Joe Pilling, Director General of the Prison Service from 1991-1993, delivering the Eve Saville Memorial Lecture at the Institute for the Study and Treatment of Delinquency in June 1992, described the Mission Statement as 'incorporating the values which I believe should guide us in our work with the people in our care'. He also attempted to outline what was meant by the word 'humanity' as 'five distinct, yet inter-related concepts: respect; fairness; individuality; care; and

33. Ibid, p65.
34. The Guardian (22nd April 1989). 'Governors claim prison plan puts public at risk'.

openness'[35]. Indeed the force of the 'moral' aspect of the Mission Statement can be gauged in the continued attempts to have it rewritten so that only its first 'security' sentence applies. This is especially apparent after high-profile escapes, or periods of disorder. A copy of the Service's Purpose, Vision, Goals and Values is contained in Appendix 1. Riots, sadly, seem always to be with us. However, during the last ten years most disorder, which had previously been the preserve of adult, male, long-term prisons became just as likely to occur in locals, remand centres, or young offender institutions. In particular the 1990 riot at HMP Manchester, which lasted 25 days and which prompted disturbances at HMPs Bristol, Cardiff and Dartmoor, brought the Prison Service under great public and political scrutiny. So great has the impact of the Manchester riot been that one leading criminologist has described it as being 'the single most significant event in modern English penal history'.[36]

This significance stems, in part, from the subsequent inquiry headed by Lord Justice Woolf as he then was, who concluded that the cause of the disturbances related to a shared sense of injustice by prisoners. The need to establish justice in prisons, a notion not dissimilar to legitimacy, led Woolf to recommend various practical changes on such things as the nature of the standard prison regime, and how prisoners should be advised about decisions which affected them. At the time there was an overwhelming unanimity of support for what became known as the 'Woolf Agenda', and much of what was proposed was readily accepted, and incorporated into the 1991 Criminal Justice Act. However, the effect that Woolf has had it still unclear and opinion remains divided over his lasting impact.[37]

Whilst riots and disorder pose distinct problems, especially if the disturbances are protracted and attract media attention, they are events which are eventually brought under control and in re-establishing that control credit is given to the Prison Service. For example, responding to a question posed about disturbances at HMP Full Sutton in January 1997, Prime Minister John Major commented that 'I am delighted that it

35. The text was reprinted in 'Perspectives on Prisons: A Collection of views on Prison Life and Running Prisons'. A Supplement of the Report on the Work of the Prison Service, April 1991-March 1992. (HMSO) (1992) pp5-11. The whole issue of 'aims', and a comparison of the English and Welsh Statement of Purchase with that of the Scottish Prison Service, can be found in AE BOTTOMS (1990) The Aims of Imprisonment, in Justice, Guilt and Forgiveness in the Penal System, Edinburgh Centre for Theology and Public Issues.

36. SPARKS (1996), op cit, p215.

37. For a recent discussion on the Impact of Woolf see SPARKS (1996), pp215-218 and I DUNBAR and A LANGDON (1998) Tough Justice, London, Blackstone.

was handled so swiftly and efficiently'.[38] Similarly Michael Howard, then Home Secretary, whilst visiting the prison after the disturbance had been quelled, commented to staff that 'I am very grateful ... for a highly professional job very well done'. He went on:

> 'Great courage was displayed by those involved in the initial stages of the incident, who had to take difficult decisions, took them quickly and calmly and by so doing prevented injury and possible loss of life.'[39]

Both the Prime Minister and the Home Secretary singled out the work of the Prison Service's National Control and Restraint (C and R) teams, specially trained staff who use unarmed techniques aimed at quelling disorder, and the co-operation between the Prison Service and the police, through the use of the former's contingency planning arrangements. Indeed what has proven harder for the Prison Service to deal with has been the prevention of escapes, especially by Category A or B prisoners.

'It was 8.10pm on Friday 9 September 1994, when the concentration of the prison officers in the Special Secure Unit (SSU) at Whitemoor prison was disrupted by a telephone call announcing that several of their charges were in the process of escaping over the prison wall.'[40] So opens the racy, damning report into the escape of six 'exceptional risk' category A prisoners, five of whom were members of the Irish Republican Army, from HMP Whitemoor. The enquiry, headed by Sir John Woodcock, a former policeman, and assisted by some 11 other policemen, has impacted on how the Prison Service operates at virtually every level. It led directly to the sacking of Derek Lewis, the Director General; the Home Secretary faced a motion of 'no confidence' but survived that, and numerous calls for his resignation; and almost every aspect of prison life from staff training and selection, to the use of dogs, inmate privileges and the transfer of their property was touched in some way. This is all the more remarkable given that whilst these changes might reasonably have been expected in the dispersal estate, they have in fact permeated into all Prison Service establishments.

38. Quoted in Prison Service News, Volume 15, No 151 January/February 1997, p1.

39. Ibid, p13.

40. Report of the Inquiry into the escape of six prisoners from the Special Secure Unit at Whitemoor Prison in Cambridgeshire on Friday 9 September 1994 (Woodcock Report (1994) Cmnd 2741: HMSO, London.

Woodcock's effect, coupled with the subsequent review of security by General Sir John Learmont, following an escape from HMP Parkhurst in 1995,[41] has been to re-establish an older set of priorities as a guiding philosophy for the Prison Service. This 'back to the future' approach has caught a popular mood, both inside and outside the Prison Service, and has resulted in a general hardening of life inside for individual inmates and severely hampered general attempts to reform the system as a whole. Indeed this process has been exacerbated by reduced budgets which has limited the numbers and work of education staff, probation officers and physical education staff who make a major contribution to a prison's regime.

Yet contemporaneously the old debate about what can be achieved in attempting to reform offenders, pessimistically characterised in the 1970s as 'nothing works'[42] has, against this hardening background, been challenged by asking 'what works'. Most notably, a far-reaching sex offender treatment programme was launched and Mark Williams, then a principal psychologist in the Prison Service, claimed that 'an integrated programme of work, education and adherence to prison routines, coupled with programmes directed at the offending behaviour as such, can have an important rehabilitational effect.'[43] Then in October 1993, presumably for very different reasons, but echoing the words of Merlyn Rees before him in the late 1970s, Michael Howard declared to the Conservative Party Conference that, after all, 'prison works'.

However, his would seem to be a message based on the incapacitative nature of imprisonment, rather than the possible rehabilitative effects of specific treatment programmes. Nonetheless by making this claim Howard placed prisons, yet again, in the public eye and as part of the political agenda.

The opposition's response was encapsulated in Tony Blair's declaration in 1994 that the Labour Party would be 'tough on crime and tough on the causes of crime'. However, in the run-up to the 1997 general election some saw both parties place an increasing emphasis

41. Review of Prison Service Security in England and Wales and the escape from Parkhurst Prison on Tuesday 3 January 1995 (Learmont Report) (1995) Cmnd 1456, HMSO, London.

42. This idea is most often associated with the work of R MARTINSON (1974) 'What Works? Questions and Answers about Prison Reform', The Prison Interest, No 35, pp22-54.

43. M WILLIAMS 'What Works?: Research and Rehabilitation in Perceptions on Prisons: A Collection of Views on Prison Life and Running Prisons, A Supplement of the Report on the Work of the Prison Service, April 1991 - March 1992 (HMSO 1992), pp16-18. For a general introduction into the treatment of sex offenders see A SAMPSON (1990) Sex Offenders in Prison, London: Prison Reform Trust.

upon the punitive rather than the rehabilitative purpose of criminal policy generally and of prisons in particular. Whatever the reported rhetoric of New Labour's approach to crime, in office it has adopted a very different approach both to the management of the Prison Service and in what it wants the Prison Service to do.

New Labour - New Directions

Part of this government's commonality with the last administration can be explained as the inevitable consequence of the re-moralisation of the politics of 'law n' order' after the murder of James Bulger in 1993, which seemed to propel both major parties into a Dutch auction of 'toughness' in relation to crime and punishment.[44] Similarly, in relation to prisons, given the practical difficulties of managing the growing prison population when they came to power, perhaps it was also inevitable that change would be slow in coming. As a consequence, the new Home Secretary approved the use of a converted ship as a prison - which had been the focus of much criticism when it had first been proposed by Michael Howard, and which is now running to full capacity off Portland harbour as HMP The Weare.

More controversially the new Home Secretary also approved of the development of Secure Training Centres (STCs), which would house 12-14 year olds - another reflection of the impact of the murder of James Bulger - the first of which was to be run by Group 4. This inevitably raised the question of New Labour's approach to prison privatisation, which had become increasingly central to the Conservative's approach to managing the penal estate. Those who were opposed to prison privatisation had seen Mr Straw's comments, in opposition, that he thought prison privatisation 'morally repugnant', as an indication of the policy direction that he would take once in power. Those who sought, as an indication of the differences between the New Labour and the Conservative party, the former's renunciation of privatisation were disappointed. However, the issue of privatisation is not the only guide as to whether this administration is different from its predecessor. It has to be acknowledged that as well as continuing the emphasis upon the Prison Service's primary duty to keep in custody those committed by the courts, the Labour government has demonstrated a commitment to

44. For further discussion of this theme, and the impact of the Bulger murder see J ASHTON and D WILSON (1998): What everyone in Britain Should Know About Crime and Punishment, London: Blackstone.

developing purposeful regimes. Following the comprehensive review of public spending, the Prison Service was given around £226 million for regime development in four key areas: offending behaviour programmes, drug misuse, education and more sharply focused and better integrated regimes for the under 18 year olds. This signalled a renewed belief in the Prison Service's rehabilitative role. The introduction of TV in cells and the earlier release of prisoners under the Home Detention Curfew scheme also reflect the different approach this administration is taking.

Meanwhile, echoes of the past keep re-emerging. In June 1999 HM Chief Inspector of Prisons, in a much leaked report about conditions at HMP Wormwood Scrubs, was scathing in his criticism of staff at the prison who are alleged to have assaulted prisoners in the segregation unit. This in turn re-kindled industrial relations difficulties, re-focused attention on the multi-dimensional needs of managing a prison, and of the special skills and qualities that are needed by prison staff of all grades.[45] The management of the prison has in turn responded with its own 118 point plan to 'turn the jail around', in an atmosphere of continued rumour, speculation, and media attention. Similarly the problem of releasing paedophiles back into a community which is less than welcoming has seen HMP Nottingham establish flats within its walls to house such offenders who have reached the end of their sentences - to howls of protest from local residents. The idea of a prison being the only safe place for people who have finished their sentence is indeed ironic and suggests that HM Prison Service might have to respond to many new challenges in the years to come.

One of the clearest indications of the direction in which New Labour is moving in relation to penal matters can be found in the prisons-probation review which proposes to establish a 'National Corrections Policy Framework'.[46] The review describes the basis of the work of prisons and probation as being 'the common nature of the enterprise'. The creation of a single ministerial post with responsibility for both prisons and probation is a recognition of this commonality.'[47] The linkage between the two Services is reflected in proposed shared objectives and the means of measuring the success in achieving them:

45. F MICHAEL (1998) 'Screwed Up', The Guardian, 22 April.

46. Home Office (1998) Joining Forces to Protect the Public - Prisons-Probation: A Consultation Document, London: Home Office.

47. Ibid, pp 15-16.

common Key Performance Indicators (KPI) 'on two crucial areas ... crime reduction and improved public protection have been identified as the primary goals of joint working between the two services, and performance against these goals should be measured'.[48]

In doing all of this the cultural differences between the two Services will need to be acknowledged. The promotion of 'public protection' as the overarching goal of both Services appears to sit more comfortably with the work of HM Prison Service than that of the Probation Service which has always seen itself as having other aims as well. A further indication of New Labour's direction in an effort to 'protect the public' can be gauged in the consultation paper 'Managing Dangerous People with Severe Personality Disorders'. This was published in July 1999 by the Department of Health and the Home Office and it could result in the Mental Health Act being amended so that people with personality disorders could be locked up, not because they were 'treatable' or because they had committed a crime, but as a consequence of the risk that they might pose to the public. The consultation paper also foresees a new specialist service being set up to manage this new group of inmates that would be separate from, but have close links to, HM Prison Service.

It is too early to judge the effect of the government's new approach to crime and prisons and too early to determine what real differences it will deliver. What is already clear is that there is among ministers, criminologists and criminal justice practitioners a growing consensus that the Prison Service can deliver something more than incarceration. The higher expectations the government and the public now have of public services and the advent of such changes as the Human Rights Act will help keep penal policy and prisons the sensitive political issue they have always been. Accordingly, the management of the Prison Service at the level of the Director General and the prison governor, will remain the complex management task Sir Raymond Lygo described it as being, and not one susceptible to simplistic definition and analysis.[49]

48. Ibid, pp 16-17.

49. SR DONZINGER (ed) (1996) The Real War on Crime: Harper Perennial. All figures quoted are taken from this book.

CHAPTER 2

GOVERNORS

> 'Generally, we would say that governors are men of limited knowledge, disciplinarians, lacking in imagination, sceptical about new proposals, but conscientious and just'[1]

> 'The Prison Service is the most complex and difficult management task I have encountered.'[2]

This chapter describes the legal basis of the office of governor and what powers the governor can exercise. How many governors are there? How are they selected and what training do they get? These, and other questions, are answered. An attempt is made to describe the roles and responsibilities of the governor, to identify what the governor of an average prison is accountable for in terms of money, staff and prisoners, and to highlight key issues which are explored in more detail later in the book.

The definition of 'governor'

The legal basis of the term governor can be traced to an Act of Parliament of 1839.[3] The Act provided that if the persons authorised by law to appoint the Gaoler or Keeper of any prison 'shall appoint such Keeper by the style of Governor such Governor shall have all the Powers and Duties of the Gaoler or Keeper of that Prison; and all Enactments made with regard to the Gaoler or Keeper shall apply to the Governor so appointed'. McConville argues that:

> 'The title 'governor' was associated with the rise in social standing of the occupation; many authorities introduced the term in an attempt to improve the dignity of the office: it would have been unthinkable, for example, to sully the sense of moral mission and social prestige of Millbank or Gloucester Penitentiaries by giving their chief officials the title of 'gaoler' or even 'keeper'. 'Governor' was evocative of deputising

1. S HOBHOUSE, F BROCKWAY (1922) English Prisons Today, London: Longman Green.
2. R LYGO (1991) Report on the Management of the Prison Service: HM Prison Service.
3. An Act for the Better Ordering of Prisons (1839), 2 + 3 Vict., c.56, s24.

duties on behalf of higher authority; an image reminiscent of colonial administration'.[4]

The focus of this book is primarily on the governing governor, the person in charge of the prison. The term governor will therefore be used in this book in reference to that role. Other, more junior governors will be referred to as governor grades. These governor grades may occupy a number of posts, including deputy governor, head of custody, head of activities and head of security, each of whom will be accountable to the governor. Some governor grades also occupy the position of Home Office 'Controller' in privately managed prisons, to monitor the performance level of the private sector against the contract specifications.

The Prison Service will introduce new pay and grading arrangements in July 2000. The effect will be to remove the title governor from all grades. Managers will be known as Prison Service Manager 1, 2 or 3. The title governor will remain for the person in charge of the establishment, the governing governor as a description of role, rather than grade.

Who is governing?

Each of the 138 or so public sector prisons in England and Wales is required to have a governor by virtue of Section 7 of the Prisons Act 1952. The rank of that governor will depend on the size and complexity of the establishment. The maximum security 'dispersal' prisons and large local remand prisons have a senior governor who will be a governor grade 1. The majority of other prisons will be governed by a governor grade 2, whereas smaller prisons will have a governor grade 3. In addition to the governor, a number of other governor grades will work in a prison. The exact number of governor grades and their ranks will vary and will be agreed between the governor and their line manager. Governors are managed by area managers. The area managers report to the Deputy Director General who sits on the Prison Service Management Board.

The Wynn-Parry Report in 1958 identified 225 governor grades in post, of whom nine per cent were women.[5] A breakdown of the present

4. S McCONVILLE (1981) A History of English Prison Administration, Vol 1, 1750-1877, p307.

5. Report of the Committee on Remuneration and Conditions of Service of Certain Grades in the Prison Service (Wynn-Parry Report) (1958), London: HMSO.

number of governor grades, their ranks and gender are shown in figure 3. The low percentage of women and ethnic minorities at senior governor grades has been a major concern of the Prison Service for some time. Despite equality of opportunity being one of the Prison Service's core values, and concerted efforts to develop and implement its own equal opportunities strategy, the number of women at the top of the Service continues to be small. However, at least half the members on the recent APS cohorts have been women. This is not true for ethnic minority representation, as few members of the APS are from ethnic minorities.

During 1996/1997 the Prison Service ran a Voluntary Early Retirement Scheme known as VERSE, in order to reduce the number of posts in the Service. The scheme was part of an overall cost reduction strategy. Its impact was great, with many experienced and able governors leaving the Service over a relatively short period of time.

Figure 3 : Governor grades in post (January 2000)

Grade	Total	Female	
		No.	per cent
Governor 1	41	3	7
Governor 2	72	10	14
Governor 3	139	26	19
Governor 4	311	47	15
Governor 5	517	64	12
Total	1080	150	14

Employment status of governors

Chapter IV of part VII of the Criminal Justice and Public Order Act 1994 was enacted to clarify the employment status of governor grades and prison officers.[6] It regulates their employment rights and the status of their trade unions and makes it illegal to induce industrial action by them.[7] As a result of the Act governors have the same rights as any other employee in relation to matters such as unfair dismissal, redundancy, maternity and access to Employment Tribunals. In order to take account

6. A more detailed consideration of the background to the Act and its importance can be found in Chapter 4.

7. A useful discussion of the legislation can be found in M WASIK and R TAYLOR (1995) Blackstone's Guide to the Criminal Justice and Public Order Act 1994, London: Blackstone Press.

of the reduced bargaining power resulting from the inability to take industrial action, section 128 of the Act provides authority for the Secretary of State to make regulations setting up procedures (after consultation) for the determination of pay and related terms and conditions of employment.

Governor grades are entitled to 30 days annual leave plus eight days public holidays and three privilege days per year. There are no specified hours which governors have to work, as governor grades are termed 'all hours worked grades'. Governors are routinely expected to work some evenings, make visits to their prisons at night (between 2300 and 0600 hours) and to work some weekends. The normal retirement age for governor grades is 60.

The pay rates for governor grades reflect the 'unsociable hours' element required in the job and are shown in figure 4.

Figure 4 : Governor Grade Pay Rates January 1999

Grade	Basic Pay (maximum)
Governor 1	£54,156
Governor 2	£48,721
Governor 3	£41,977
Governor 4	£36,055
Governor 5	£32,295

An additional allowance of £2,250 is paid to those governor grades working in central London.

The pay rates are less than the salaries paid to directors of contracted out prisons. A recently advertised Prison Director post, which equated with a governor grade 2 post, had a salary quoted at £80,000 plus company car, private health care and pension scheme.

Recruitment, selection and training of new entrants to the governor grade

Governors are often asked by members of the public (and indeed, by Home Office officials) why they joined the Prison Service. This is usually followed by questions about how does someone become a governor, and what qualifications are needed.

In the early part of the twentieth century governors were appointed by the Home Secretary and their subordinate officers by the Prison Commissioners. Hobhouse and Brockway recorded, in 1922, that:

> 'On what principles the selection of governors is made it would be difficult to say. No particular qualifications are demanded by law, and the frequency with which retired military and naval officers are appointed indicates that disciplinary capacity is primarily considered. Some of the appointments suggest that the influence of highly placed persons has been effective. Of the 54 prison governors, 26 have served with the regular forces.'[8]

Appointment to the post of governor was at the time the result of influence, grace and favour. Colonel C E F Rich made it clear that his appointment to the Prison Service was the result of merciless lobbying by such high ranking acquaintances as Sir John Dickson-Poynder, later Lord Islington, who approached the chairman of the Prison Commission on Rich's behalf, and a friendly Duke who went to see the Home Secretary.[9] As a result, and following a cursory medical examination and a modicum of training, Rich was appointed deputy governor of Wakefield Prison.

The Hobhouse and Brockway Report was also highly critical of the military characteristics of governors even though it recognised that military and naval training undoubtedly develops capacity for organisation and maintenance of discipline. The Report suggested that the 'model' governor would have the qualifications of both the educationalist and the psychologist and that it was 'inexcusable that governors should be so ignorant of their subject'.

Sir Maurice Waller, on his appointment as chairman of the Prison Commission, did all in his power to give effect to the recommendations of the Report, and, in 1922, was responsible for appointing Alexander Paterson as a Prison Commissioner. The appointment of Paterson, an official in the Ministry of Labour, to the Commission was a clear signal that things were going to change. Paterson devoted much time and prodigious effort to staff recruitment, training and promotion. The impact made by Paterson can be seen in B D Grew's account of his recruitment as a governor.

---

8. HOBHOUSE and BROCKWAY (1922), op cit, p362.

9. CEF RICH (1932) Recollections of a Prison Governor, London: Hurst and Blackett. For a useful commentary on Rich's book see P QUINN (1994) Managing Prisons in a Time of Change: The Visions and Values of Colonel Rich, The Criminologist, vol 17, p110.

'I saw the advertisement in *The Times*. 'Housemasters and Deputy Governors wanted in HM Prison Service' it said, and ran into two or three inches to describe the minimum qualifications, the pay and prospects ... I sent in my application. A few days later a letter from the Home Office invited me to attend an interview before a Selection Board.'[10]

The recruitment structure for governors changed little in subsequent decades. People were selected through the Civil Service Commission, underwent a period of training and then took up post as a junior governor grade. In more recent years, recruits aged 24 and under were required to spend one year serving as a prison officer before joining the assistant governor training programme whereas recruits aged over 24 years were required to spend only three months as a prison officer. Prison officers could apply to become assistant governors and, if successful, at the Civil Service Commission Board, would join the next available assistant governors' training programme. The first assistant governors' course took place in 1946 and figure 5 shows the number recruited as assistant governors each year between 1973 and 1987.

Figure 5 : Number of Assistant Governors recruited each year since 1973

Year	Number of People
1973	25
1974	31
1975	30
1976	22
1977	22
1978	27
1979	24
1980	25
1981	30
1982	32
1983	25
1984	28
1985	28
1986	19
1987	9

The direct entry assistant governor scheme, which was based on the military model of directly recruiting to the officer rank, ended in 1987.

10. BD GREW (1958) Prison Governor, London: Herbert Jenkins.

Today there are four routes to becoming a governor grade. The main route is on promotion from principal officer, the most senior uniformed grade. Existing principal officers who have demonstrated the necessary competence to become a governor grade are recommended by their line manager and attend an assessment centre. If successful, new governors attend a two-week new governor 5 course and apply for vacancies. The APS is the second route and is aimed at graduates and exceptional existing staff. The scheme provides members with a wide range of experience and training and gives them the opportunity to reach senior management in less than five years. The third route is the Direct Entry Scheme aimed at experienced managers from inside and outside the Prison Service. Applicants must have at least five years management experience in a dynamic people orientated organisation. The final route of entry is the Cross-Hierarchy Move Scheme which is aimed at existing civil servants. It seeks talented staff in other occupational groups who are skilled individuals with a flair for managing people and who are looking to develop and further their careers within an operational setting.

Applicants for all schemes undertake written tests, attend a Job Simulation Assessment Centre (JSAC) and are the subject of an extended interview process. Successful candidates who have no experience as prison officers are required to pass prison officer training and then to spend a period as a prison officer. On completion of the period in uniform they then undertake a prison management course and normally achieve accreditation, to governor 5, 12 to 24 months later.

Promotion from one governor grade to the next depends on developing the requisite competency, skills and knowledge, favourable recommendations from line management and attendance at assessment centres. Promotion to an in charge governor post requires experience in a number of different types of prisons, attendance on a variety of courses and in most cases, experience as a deputy governor.

The type of person and qualities needed to become a governor grade has varied over time. The recruitment literature for 1967 reads: 'Duties demand a lively interest in social problems and a good understanding of modern methods of handling them'. By 1969 this had been changed to 'Are you interested in social work? Could you also - with the right training - do a good managerial job?' The emphasis had switched dramatically by the time of the 1972 advertisement:

> 'Management within a Social Purpose: As an assistant governor you are primarily a manager. You will organise, train and support the staff through whom you are responsible for the entire existence of a group of offenders in custody. As you may have to deal personally with the problems of your charges, you must be able to recognise their needs and have knowledge of the specialist skills and resources available for their treatment and rehabilitation.'[11]

The 1997 recruitment literature for the APS reveals how far the pendulum has now moved from the social work emphasis of the 1960s:

> 'Being a prison governor is probably the most complicated people management task you will ever come across. The daily challenges of the Prison Service are immense. Maintaining a balance between our duty to protect the public by keeping offenders securely in custody and our duty to help people in prison address their problems is never easy. Add to this a commitment to our staff and to the effective use of resources and you'll begin to appreciate just what the job involves.
> That's why the people we recruit onto the APS have got to be exceptional. We welcome graduates from any discipline, and from any race, ethnic origin, religion or gender, because we're only interested in your personal qualities and abilities. Stamina, enthusiasm, leadership, organisational flair, numerical and analytical ability should accompany strong interpersonal skills, but without plenty of self confidence you'll never make it.'

The role of the Governor

What then do governors do? The answer to this question is explored in the remaining chapters of this book. However, at this stage, it is useful to try and capture the essence of governing in order to provide a framework and to identify themes which are developed in subsequent chapters.

The Wynn-Parry Report of 1958 summarised the role of the governor as follows:

11. Quoted in PA WADDINGTON (1983) The Training of Prison Governors - Role, Ambiguity and Socialisation, London: Croom Helm.

'The governor is responsible to the [Secretary of State] for everything that goes on in his establishment: the principle aspects of his work are the maintenance of security, good order and discipline; the leadership of those sections of his staff more closely concerned with the training of the inmates, and the direction of their efforts to this end; the co-ordination of the various departments within the establishment; the development of useful activity in work, education and recreation; co-operation with outside bodies such as the education authority and with voluntary agencies and workers; and responsibility, as sub-accounting officer, for the proper use of public money and property.'[12]

The role of governor had been translated, by 1994, to that of 'general manager of an establishment, emphasising the need to understand specialist areas as well as a need to think and plan strategically'.[13] This move to managerialism is reflected in a more comprehensive overview of the role and function of the governor provided by EDMC Management Consultants. Their observations are recounted at length given that it is a relatively recent 'outsiders' view of what governors are asked to do:

'Overall, the role of the governor is to manage the establishment in a safe, humane and orderly way to achieve its purpose as expressed in the contract with the area manager. This is done through visible leadership, creating and communicating a vision of the future and setting and maintaining the ethos, standards and morality of the establishment and managing the boundaries with other organisations. A key task is to develop and motivate the senior management team, to delegate functions to them, and through them to all levels in the establishment to deal with the functions of operations, security, regimes, personnel, finance, industries and farms, works services etc. Governors also assist multi-disciplinary and multi-level teams in working together in harmony to achieve these aims.

12. Report of the Committee on Remuneration and Conditions of Service of Certain Grades in the Prison Service (Wynn-Parry Report) (1958), London HMSO.

13. Prison Service Advice to Governors 26/1994.

Vital functions which set the management of prisons apart from other complex organisations are the maintenance of secure custody, care with humanity and the provision of opportunities for prisoners to address their offending behaviour - all in a setting of frequently dangerous and/or disturbed people, most of whom are confined against their will. Governors and their staff have to devise and implement regimes which reconcile the essentially contradictory issues of custodial care with opportunities for development and at the same time manage resources, staff and finances.

In line with devolution of authority from HQ, governors devise appropriate methods for the initiation and continued development of strategic plans which interpret the Service Purpose, Vision and Goals and Values and inform the ongoing life of the establishment and, crucially, provide justification for current and future funding. Governors, in common with all senior managers, need to resist the temptation of being 'sucked in' to the detail of day to day matters, despite the expectation of many that they can 'do all and know all!'

Governors continually maintain a command mode, mostly in the background, but ready at a moment's notice to be brought into effect. This quasi-military state is most visible during serious incidents. The managerial role changes to command - a state reliant on meticulous contingency planning and highly disciplined processes designed to minimise harm to staff and prisoners, and loss or damage to property. Equally, the command mode can be employed as a preventive measure if equilibrium is threatened. Since most governors are not continually dealing with serious incidents, great emphasis is laid on planning, practice and training, either informally, on the job, or through the valued simulation training provided by the Prison Service College.

Governors spend much time in negotiating agreements with a wide variety of players - area managers, specialist departments, colleagues, governing governors, senior management team and employee representatives. Underpinning values to this are the creation of situations of mutual advantage (win-win) though this may not always be reciprocated by others.

Governors continually balance a wide range of frequently contradictory functions; the tension between custody and care is at the heart of everything they do. In these, mostly stressful situations, governors need to find or develop adequate support mechanisms to help deal with their own anxieties.

Governors represent their establishment to the media, local community, other parts of the criminal justice system, and to HQ. In this they need particular skills in dealing with the media, since supportive interviewing and objective reporting cannot be guaranteed. They also act as representatives of the state to prisoners and in discharging this role they adjudicate breaches of prison discipline. Despite this 'exposure' to a wide range of interactions, much of the governor's decision making process is marked by loneliness.

Much of a governor's energies are expended in assessing and managing risk and making decisions about people's lives. Often this is done in the absence of adequate information and a judgement has to be made about gaining more information, but the timescale of the prison system pressures them, raising further personal conflicts which have to be mediated.

A less easily described aspect of the governor role is the management of people - both staff and prisoners - who may be in highly charged emotional states, where an ill considered management word or action can precipitate violence or tragedy. This calls for a particularly sensitive awareness of the psychological state of others.'[14]

The Prison Service Review published in 1997 recommended that the Prison Service draw up an up-to-date role definition of the job of the governor. By late 1999 there had been no agreement on the content of the role definition. This reflects its complexity and the various perspectives and expectations people have of the governor. The description outlined below was generated by Chris Roden and Shane Bryans during the debate about the role of the governor but was never accepted by the Prison Service Management Board.

Governors need to be resilient and knowledgeable people with a wide range of skills. The governor must provide both staff and

14. Training Needs of Governing Governors and Others in HM Prison Service of England and Wales (1995), HM Prison Service.

prisoners with strong professional leadership that can enable the establishment and the Service as a whole to deliver objectives set by ministers. The role of the governor is challenging. It requires personal commitment and the ability to deal effectively with competing demands. The governor is required to maximise resources to protect the public and reduce crime. The work is accomplished with and through people; therefore, many of the skills needed are those associated with general management. However, the role goes further: the governor must appreciate the political sensitivities and public concerns surrounding prisons and understand the sometimes volatile or fragile nature of prison culture. Occasionally the role requires calmness and courage in the face of violent disorder. It is possible to identify four elements to the role of the governor: leading; interpreting; resourcing and representing

a. Leading

A governor's ability to influence events is integrally linked to the quality of relationships that they form and develop with other people, and the way they exercise their authority. This is the key to shared ownership of and commitment to driving the establishment forward and building on success. The governor must recognise the potential in the senior team, and use it to empower and develop all staff to ensure the establishment meets set key performance targets within the allocated budget, while maintaining a proper balance between custody, care and rehabilitation. This requires visible leadership for both staff and prisoners, particularly where defensible decisions need to be made in complex and difficult situations. It follows that the role of the governor can be extremely demanding. An understanding of social relations and the dynamics of personal relationships is central to managing the complexity of a total institution, especially when trying to effect change. Prisons are about people and emotions. Therefore, the governor must understand and work with the emotions within a prison. Governors need to be sensitive to what they hear, feel and see in managing the tensions created by the conflicting value systems. The atmosphere should be that of a committed but not oppressive environment where staff and prisoners work together in a range of purposeful activities. To maintain a balance between the legitimate expectations of staff and prisoners, it is vital that governors set boundaries to ensure that bullying, predatory behaviour and trafficking are kept to a minimum. The governor needs to guard against abuse of power and ensure that staff exercise their authority legitimately and fairly. It is, therefore, essential that staff be trained to manage prisoners sensitively but firmly, and with confidence.

b. Interpreting

The governor is the person who has a total overview of the prison and its place within the wider framework of the criminal justice system and Home Office. Governors are faced with the difficulty of reconciling the conflict between the various penal objectives, political expediency, humanity and expectations of various stakeholders both in and out of the establishment. Negotiating a shared understanding of policies and the functions of the establishment is also important. There has to be a marrying of the 'management of the boundaries' and the 'management of the establishment'; the establishment cannot operate in a social vacuum. The governor must be aware of the interaction and the interdependency between the two.

c. Resourcing

The governor is responsible for seeking, utilising and maximising resources for the establishment. This is achieved by lobbying area managers and headquarters policy groups to obtain routine and project funding. The governor has to be fully aware of resource opportunities beyond the boundaries (for example) joint ventures and partnerships, which can enable the establishment to move forward and create positive change. The challenge for the governor is to achieve the key performance targets and to deliver better outcomes against a background of infinite demands and limited resources.

d. Representing

The governor is a public figure who represents the establishment in the community, to the media and at official functions with local dignitaries. Occasionally the governor may represent the establishment, Prison Service and Home Office when contributing to both European and international penal policy making. The governor also represents the establishment to the rest of the Prison Service through attendance at Headquarters, area meetings and local criminal justice forums. Governors are often the most senior Prison Service or Home Office manager with whom many staff will come into contact. They may be required to make presentations to staff and prisoners and to attend funerals and commemorative ceremonies.

Legal status of the governor

What then is the legal status of the prison governor? Section 7(1) of the Prison Act 1952 (as amended) states that 'every prison shall have a governor, a chaplain and a medical officer and such other officers as may be necessary'. The office of prison governor is therefore a creation of statute and the powers of the governor are original and not derived from, or exercised on behalf of, the Home Secretary. The Home Secretary, under S47 of the Act, can make 'rules for the management of prisons, remand centres, young offender institutions and secure training centres'. These rules are to be found as Prison Rules 1999 and the Young Offender Institution Rules 1988 (as amended) and control the extent of the governor's power. All references hereafter are to the Prison Rules unless otherwise stated.

The Act itself specifies very little about the duties of the governor except that he or she must:

- tell prisoners which employees are authorised to conduct searches (S8A(4));
- record prisoners' religion on reception (S10);
- bring any entry in the visitors' book to the attention of the board of visitors (S19).

The Prison Rules 1999 give to the governor a number of independent powers - including the powers:

- to search officers of the prison (R64);
- to change the recorded religious denomination of a prisoner (R13);
- to stop any letter or communication on the ground that its contents are objectionable or that it is of inordinate length (R34 (4));
- to allow extra letters (R35 (3));
- to defer the right of a prisoner to a visit until the expiration of any period of cellular confinement (R35 (5));
- to open, read or stop correspondence with legal advisers subject to provisions within the Rules (R39A)
- to confiscate any unauthorised article found in the possession of a prisoner, or concealed or deposited anywhere within a prison (R43 (5));
- to segregate a prisoner for a period of up to three days (R45);

- ✦ to confine temporarily in a special cell a refractory or violent prisoner (R48);
- ✦ to authorise compulsory testing for controlled drugs (R50);
- ✦ to adjudicate and award punishment to prisoners (R53 (2)) and 55);
- ✦ to remove from a prison any person who does not leave when required to do so (R71(2)).

However, the mere fact that content is given to the governor's functions and duties by the Prison Rules does not derogate from the governor's discrete status under the Act. The importance of this distinction can be found in Lord Bridge's dicta which highlighted the issue in relation to the governor's adjudicatory powers:

> 'A prison governor may, in general terms, be aptly described as the servant of the Secretary of State, but he is not acting as such when adjudicating upon a charge of a disciplinary nature. He is then exercising the independent power conferred on him by the rules. The Secretary of State has no authority to direct the governor, as to how to adjudicate on a particular charge or what punishment should be awarded. If a Home Office official sought to stand behind the governor at a disciplinary hearing and tell him what to do, the governor would properly send him packing.'[15]

These powers are explicitly given to the governor, whilst others are given to the Secretary of State to exercise. The Secretary of State may well delegate his powers under the Prison Rules to his officials, including the governor. In turn, the governors may, under R81, with the leave of the Secretary of State, delegate any of their powers and duties under the Prison Rules to another officer of that prison. In addition, Rule 2 defines governor as 'including an officer for the time being in charge of a prison'.

The Prison Rules also confer on the governor a number of duties including:

- ✦ hearing any requests and complaints (R11);

15. Leech v Deputy Governor, Parkhurst Prison (1988) 1AC533 at 563.

- informing a prisoner's relatives if a prisoner dies, becomes seriously ill, sustains any severe injury or is removed to outside hospital on account of mental disorder (R22 (1));
- inform the coroner, board of visitors, Secretary of State, if a prisoner dies (R22 (2)).

The Prison Act makes no reference to other governor grades other than stating in S7(3) that a prison which in the opinion of the Secretary of State is large enough to require it may have a deputy governor. In law, therefore, there is no difference between a governor grade (other than the governor) and any other 'officer of a prison'. As has been pointed out elsewhere, the term 'officer of a prison' is not defined in the Act.[16] Consistent with the sketchy nature of the Act, there is no detailed exposition of the powers and duties of the various officers of a prison. This is left to the Prison Rules save in one respect. Section 8 states that 'every prison officer while acting as such shall have the powers, authority, protection and privileges of a constable'.

The legal obligations of the governor, as a public sector manager, are dealt with in Chapter 3.

Job Description

There is no standard job description for governors outlining their tasks and duties. Some attempts were made to produce one in 1984 and again in 1998. The 1998 draft version is shown below but was never accepted by the Prison Service Management Board.

a. Job Purpose

To ensure effective execution of the sentences of the courts so as to reduce re-offending and protect the public.

b. Core Principles

To ensure that the actions of the establishment comply with the policies of Ministers and the law. To protect the public by holding those committed by the courts in a safe, decent and healthy environment. To reduce crime by providing constructive regimes which address offending behaviour, improve educational and work skills and promote law-abiding behaviour in custody and after release.

16. S LIVINGSTONE and T OWEN: Prison Law - Text and Materials (1999), Oxford: Clarendon Press. 2nd Edition.

c. **Managing the Establishment**

Managing the Business

1. Through the business planning process deliver the service agreed with the area manager to achieve key performance targets.
2. Track progress and development against key performance targets and demonstrate this on a monthly basis.
3. Assess and address the implications of any changes to the required service and/or the level of resources.
4. Ensure that financial control mechanisms are in place and that decisions taken about the use of resources reflect the need to ensure value for money and continuous growth.
5. Create and implement a self-audit system to ensure the agreed processes and outputs are being delivered in accordance with the relevant legislation, standards, orders and instructions, thereby to ensure compliance and meet the required rating when audited.
6. Develop and test comprehensive contingency plans to ensure the successful command and resolution of any serious incident.

Managing Staff and Prisoners

7. Ensure that standards of behaviour conform to statute, code of conduct and discipline and the Prison Service Principles.
8. Maintain order and discipline amongst prisoners.
9. Ensure communication systems are in place for staff, prisoners and visitors to the establishment.
10. Maintain proper discipline amongst staff and ensure there are procedures for occupational health and safety, staff support, grievances, disciplinary action and employee relations, including relationships with trade unions.
11. Provide constructive regimes for prisoners that reduce re-offending by improving basic literacy, numeracy and work skills, providing programmes that address offending behaviour and by reducing drug misuse.
12. Manage the senior management team and through them empower all staff to meet the objectives of the establishment.

Managing the boundaries

13. Work constructively with agencies, both statutory and voluntary in order to ensure that the establishment makes an

effective contribution to the criminal justice system by reducing crime and protecting the public.

14. Anticipate, respond to and manage the concerns of the board of visitors.
15. Foster and pursue positive and effective public relations.

The most recent instruction on the duties of the governor is set out in Prison Service Standing Order 3A, last amended in 1985. Given the age of the standing order and the lack of recent updating, few governors will refer or even follow it. The Order deals with completing the governor's journal; the issuing of governor's orders; reporting incidents; annual reports; absence from prison; general duties; dealing with prison property; communicating with the Home Office about prisoners; elections and walking the boundary.

The Deputy Director General, Phil Wheatley, provided his view of what governors should be doing, in a speech to the Prison Service Conference in February 2000. He highlighted the complexity of the governor's job and identified three parts to it : organising the internal environment; managing processes and output, and managing the external environment, the key elements of which are explored more fully below.

a. Organising the internal environment

- Discipline and control.
- Security.
- Staff recruitment and leadership.
- Communications.
- Maintenance and development of the prison.
- Industrial relations.

b. Managing Processes and Outputs

- Budget management.
- Setting and achieving targets.
- Using management information correctly.
- Decision making.
- Driving and controlling change.
- Procurement.
- Green issues and energy management.
- Giving 'technical advice'.

c. **Managing the external environment**

- ✦ Representing the prison to the wider public.
- ✦ Forming working relationships with other agencies.
- ✦ Sensitivity to the political climate.
- ✦ Media awareness.
- ✦ Keeping alert to changes in the wider community.

Training of senior prison governors

Prior to 1981, although the police, fire service and armed services all had their command courses, there was no concept of comprehensive command training in the Prison Service. Prison governors were introduced, at the outset of their careers, to the role of the Prison Service generally and to that of the assistant governor in particular through the assistant governor course at the Prison Service College.[17] However, they were expected to acquire appropriate knowledge, skills and ability to manage a prison as the governor through experience at lower governor grade levels.

The origin of the command course for governors may be traced to the report of the May Committee of 1979.[18] The Committee, as has been explained, was set up as a means of handling a particularly fraught industrial relations issue, but in practice its terms of reference enabled it to cover a much broader field. May was critical of, and made constructive recommendations about, many aspects of Prison Service organisation and practice. In particular, the Report made recommendations for changes in management structure and style, in financial systems and in training.

The Committee accepted the evidence of the Governors' Branch of the Society of Civil and Public Servants that governors required more comprehensive training than they presently received throughout their service. Such training should include issues of public relations, management, administration and industrial relations. Elsewhere in the Report, May states 'the training of governors must be fuller and longer than it presently is'. This should be seen in the light of May's more general criticisms of the lack of status and importance attached to training within the then Prison Department as a whole.

17. For an account of the socialisation process which took place during the Assistant Governor Training see PA WADDINGTON (1983). The Training of Prison Governors: Role, Ambiguity and Socialisation, London: Croom Helm.

18. Committee of Inquiry into the United Kingdom Prison Service's Report 1979 (May Report). Cmnd 7673, London: HMSO.

During the discussions which preceded the establishment of the command course, the level at which the course would be pitched and the stage in the careers of governors at which it should be experienced received a great deal of attention. Initially, the intention had been to introduce the course for governors 4 with a view to incorporating a form of assessment which would have contributed to decisions about suitability for promotion. However, the problems associated with this approach proved insurmountable and the course was eventually developed as a post-promotion course for recently promoted governors 3. In theory at least the course was designed with governing governor skills and responsibilities in mind. This was appropriate when it was intended to assess course members' abilities in these respects, but may not have been appropriate for a course the majority of whose members would not be governing governors for several years.

The first five command courses for prison governors took place between 1983 and 1986. These courses were evaluated by Derek Williamson, of the University of Leeds and academic advisor to the Prison Service College.[19] Williamson recommended that the command course, as it was then structured, should be abandoned and replaced by a set of modules providing training in discrete skills and areas of responsibility and a new management course. This new management course was intended to meet the needs of governors of any grade about to take charge of an establishment for the first time.

By 1987 the command course had been transformed into the senior command studies programme (SCS), the eligibility criteria for which had been amended to include non-governors (SCS5 included four medical officers and SCS6 included two grades 7 from elsewhere in the civil service). The aims of the programme had also changed emphasis and were more focused on giving an opportunity for personal and professional development.

As part of a wider review of the Prison Service, the Prisons Board decided, in July 1989, to commission a review of training. A decision was taken by the Training Review Group, during 1990, that the senior command studies programme should be terminated and be replaced by a new senior management programme beginning in 1992. The thinking behind this decision appears to have been a desire to move to a more generic approach to management training, both in terms of those

19. D WILLIAMSON (1986) Evaluation of Command Courses 1983-1986, Prison Service Library.

participating in the training and in its content. The change in course content and language from 'command' to 'management' reflected the importation of the new public management ethos into the Prison Service (the rise of managerialism is discussed in Chapter 3).

Given the generic nature of the course a decision was made to contract out the provision of the programme to a university business school. The contract was awarded to De Montfort Business School in 1992 and they ran the programme until the last SMP (SMP7) in 1997. Given the changed nature of the SMP, with little emphasis on equipping people to govern prisons, the training review group decided, during 1990, to introduce a course for governors about to take charge of a prison for the first time

Courses were run in 1992 and 1993 but the lack of support meant that by 1994 no command course existed to train prison governors to govern. In order to meet this shortfall, a command course was reintroduced for new governors in 1997. It was structured around a two-week module. The conceptual basis for the course was to: acquire knowledge; provide an opportunity to explore, think and reflect; focus on 'soft skills'; gain experience in some technical area; learn techniques; and to consider behaviours and competencies required of governors. A more detailed exposition of the existing training for governors can be found in an article by Shane Bryans, 'Management Training and Development in the Prison Service'.[20]

International perspective on governors

There is no binding international legislation on the selection, duties and responsibilities of governors. However, the United Nations' Standard Minimum Rules for the Treatment of Prisoners, which were adopted in 1955, deal not only with prison conditions and prisoners' treatment, but also with staff. Rule 50 states:

> 'The director of an institution should be adequately qualified for his task by character, administrative ability, suitable training and experience.
> He shall devote his entire time to his official duties and shall not be appointed on a part-time basis.

20. S BRYANS (1999) Management Training and Development in the Prison Service, Prison Service Journal No 121, January 1999 pp27-28.

He shall reside on the premises of the institution or in its immediate vicinity.'

Penal Reform International's handbook on international good practice makes a number of comments on the qualities of good governors and what they should do.

'Two capabilities seem crucial to a prison director, acting in an essentially hierarchical and rather formally regulated institution, namely a sense of democratic and humane leadership and being an inspirational, motivating person. Partly it is a matter of personality, partly it can and should be developed by highly qualified training. A director should know how to run an organisation, be well versed in the legal system, understand how society functions and be aware of the prison's place in society. A director should also be conscious of his or her position as a role model. Subject matters which the director considers important usually will be regarded as important by the staff, and issues which the director considers unimportant will be neglected by the staff. On the one hand, the director should monitor his or her personnel, while on the other he or she should foster an open attitude which allows staff a degree of creativity in the performance of their duties. A director should be a visible figure within the prison, maintaining formal and informal contacts with his staff. He or she should listen to problems, and solve them to the best of his or her ability, whilst at the same time demonstrating a critical attitude and ensuring that staff do their work properly. He or she should keep an eye on the way officers work, and stamp out any abuses.

Prison directors should show a willingness to speak to prisoners, treating them first and foremost as human beings entitled to respect. If the pressure of work prevents them from personally seeing prisoners, a deputy should be appointed to take over this task and submit a report of prisoners' complaints and needs. Where possible and within reason, complaints should be dealt with speedily and fairly. Directors should protect the interests of prisoners in the prison, acting for them in situations involving the staff or the world outside prison. In their actions directors should be guided by the notion that it is in the interests of both prisoners and society to reduce to a minimum the difference between life in detention and life in society. Directors should ensure that the organisation's interests are served in the sense that they should make every effort to obtain from the central authority such funds as are necessary to allow the organisation to function properly.'[21]

Prison Governors' Association

The Prison Governors' Association was formed in 1987 as an independent trade union to represent all governor grades in England and Wales. In 1989 it was joined by those in Northern Ireland and today has around 1000 members representing almost 90 per cent of governor grades. Members carry out the full range of tasks from governing prisons to advising on policy at headquarters and providing support functions in prisons and headquarters.

In addition to being an independent trade union the PGA always commented on the direction of penal policy and worked to bring about change in the system for the benefit of the public and the prisoner. One example of the PGA's attempts to influence penal policy was its 1995 document titled 'A Manifesto for Change'. The document set out the PGA's views on a wide range of matters within the Prison Service and related criminal justice areas. It provided a broad-based policy which if taken as a whole would have significantly changed the way prisons were run. The PGA also made a major contribution to the Woolf Inquiry into the April 1990 Prison Disturbances, which helped to set the agenda for the Prison Service in the following decade.

The reduction in the size of the prison population prior to 1993 was in part due to PGA lobbying about overcrowding in the wake of the 1990 riots. It is clear that PGA views on community prisons, prison discipline, incentives and temporary release were also seen as significant by both ministers and the Home Affairs Select Committees. However, PGA views increasingly became less important to the Conservative Home Secretary, Michael Howard, in the mid 1990s. Media interviews with the PGA became focused on conflicts arising from the Government's 'Prison Works' policy, whereas PGA relations with the Labour Opposition were good. Some of what is now becoming

21. Penal Reform International (1995) Making Standards Work - An International Handbook on Good Prison Practice. PRI London.

penal policy was contained in the PGA Manifesto. On coming to power in 1997, Jack Straw even asked the PGA to do some research on remand times and prisoners with mental health problems.

The PGA continue to give evidence to select committees and are one of the organisations that must be consulted by the Sentencing Advisory Panel. The prisons and probation minister Paul Boateng has made it clear that he will continue to turn to the PGA for their professional views on penal affairs and penal reform and he meets with them quarterly.

Line management of governors

There have been at least 16 reviews bearing on the management and organisation of the Prison Service in the last 30 years. Many of these have had something to say about the management of governors and, cumulatively, they account for the current area manager structure.

In 1970 the Prison Service was re-organised from a centrally managed entity into four regions, with the expectation that greater devolution would help improve the general management efficiency of the Prison Service and, in particular, establish clearer lines of authority and responsibility. Each region was led by a Regional Director who sat on the Prisons Board and worked with a team operating from offices in their regions. Following major changes to working arrangements agreed under 'Fresh Start' in 1984 (and a headquarters reorganisation in 1980), the structure above establishment level also came under scrutiny. As a result, in 1988 a major organisational review by a joint Prison Service and PA Consulting Group team led by William Fittall took place. The report considered that:

- Regions had failed to provide a satisfactory linkage between policy and operations and, moreover, had not provided clear and effective line management above establishment level;
- A particular weakness was the apparent tendency of many regional staff to regard their role as being to 'support or advise' rather than manage their governors. Similarly the Regional Director spans of command of 25-39 establishments were regarded as 'impossibly wide';
- In addition, the management of the inmate population needed to be improved by eliminating awkward operational overlaps between Regional Directors and other senior staff.

The Review therefore concluded that the Prison Service needed a new structure to enable it to operate with maximum efficiency and effectiveness as a single, cohesive national organisation which brought policy and operations together at the centre and was able to be held properly accountable to ministers and Parliament. To achieve this it recommended the creation of three directorates each with operational and policy responsibilities and geographical groupings of 9-10 establishments under 15 area managers who would be based centrally within these directorates, each with a policy portfolio. The position of area manager was formally created in 1991 and the 15 posts filled at governor 1 level or, if responsible for governors 1, by Civil Service grades 5.

The Prison Service Review published in late 1997 considered the role of the area manager both in the context of the debate over geographical versus functional organisation (paragraphs 7.1-7.16), and improving business and performance management (paragraphs 8.52-8.54). It did not recommend a move away from the current geographical area structure towards the functional model advocated, for example, by Her Majesty's Chief Inspector of Prisons, noting that Prisons Probation Review would touch on this subject. It also agreed with previous reviews that the area manager system is a considerable improvement on the regional system that preceded it and that it provided greater direction and support to governors than hitherto. However, it concluded that their effectiveness was inhibited by the general weaknesses of Prison Service management systems - particularly limitations in strategic planning, IT, conflicting standards and management training.

The present arrangements therefore provide one area manager for 10 12 prisons. Each governor is managed by an assistant director who is available for support and advice. However, the primary role of the area manager is to manage governors in order to ensure that the establishment meets its key performance indicators and delivers the contents of its business plan. The area manager sets annual targets, the budget and monitors development for each establishment. The area managers themselves are now managed by a single 'operational' director, the Deputy Director General, who regularly monitors the performance of each establishment at a monthly bilateral with each area manager.

The area boundaries were amended in April 2000 to impose alignment with other criminal justice agencies and the nine

Government Offices for the Regions and Wales. There are now 12 area managers who manage establishments grouped by police areas within the boundaries of the nine English Regions. Three regions - the South East, the North West and East Midlands - have two area managers each. The 13th area manager manages the three prisons in Wales. In addition, there are two Functional Managers, a Director for the High Security Prisons and a Director who manages the female estate.

Governors are few in number, have a unique role and only occupy a high profile when things go wrong. The complexity of the job and the competency needed to do it well are not generally understood. Confusion continues to exist about the best approach to adopt for the training and development of governors. Yet much of this confusion over the recruitment and training of governors is caused by the lack of clarity about their role and what skills and abilities are needed to govern effectively. The following chapters attempt to shed some light on these key areas.

CHAPTER 3

UNDERSTANDING GOVERNING

> 'Prevailing intellectual discourses and political ideologies will have a substantial impact on a penal system, yet it is equally possible to suppose that the initiative and energy of individual actors can do much to shape prisons within those constraints'.[1]

Prisons as unique institutions

Prisons are frequently described as 'total institutions' which are similar in nature to hospitals, mental asylums and military barracks. Whilst prisons share some characteristics with other total institutions, we would argue that a number of factors specific to prisons make them unique. The first is that prisoners are forced to be in prison against their will. An element of compulsion exists. Hospital patients and military personnel voluntarily reside in their institutions in the majority of cases.[2] Secondly, the power disparity between staff and prisoners is far greater than between hospital staff and patients or between military staff and recruits. Sparks et al, in their study of dispersal prisons, point out that the dialectic of domination and subordination is very different in prison compared to other institutions and that prisoners' dependency is likewise more pronounced.[3] Thirdly, the level of deprivation imposed on people in prison is far greater than that imposed on people in other institutions. In addition to the loss of liberty, prisoners are deprived of sexual relations with partners, freedom of movement and ability to purchase many items. Fourthly, the level of surveillance is much higher in prison. Privacy is non-existent as prisoners can be watched at all times, including whilst using toilet and shower facilities, and whilst meeting families or friends in the visits area. Finally, the control of all activity in a custodial institution is inherently high. Prisoners have no choice about when to work, exercise, eat or the times at which they are locked in their cells. Visits, recreation and education are all set down in a controlled regime.

---

1. B FORSYTHE (1990) Foucault's Carceral and Ignatieff's Pentonville — English Prisons and the Revisionist Analysis of Control and Penalty. Policy and Society, Vol pp141-158.
2. Notable exceptions include patients who are detained in psychiatric hospitals against their will and conscripts who are forced to remain in their barracks.
3. R SPARKS, A BOTTOMS, W HAY (1996) Prisons and the Problem of Order, Oxford University Press. See also G RICHARDSON (1994) 'From Rights to Expections' in E PLAYER and M JENKINS (eds) Prisons after Woolf, London: Routledge.

These five factors make prisons *sui generis*.[4] The governing of these unique institutions has traditionally been seen as being unlike any other managerial or administrative job. However, the view that public sector competencies are distinct from private sector competencies has recently been challenged.

Public and private sector competencies

There is a strongly held view amongst some commentators that there is, or should be, something fundamentally different about the way public services are managed, and that generic managerial competencies are not valid across the public/private sector divide. Stewart and Ranson suggest that, whilst specific management tools are transferable, the model of management is not the same in the public and private sector. They adopt a differentials approach and argue for recognition of 'the distinct purposes, conditions and tasks of the public domain and the dilemmas which they raise for management'.[5] A number of examples of this 'distinctness' are quoted, including financial management and budgetary process and accountability. In the public sector increased demand for the product or service does not necessarily result in an increase in supply; the NHS would be one such example. Management in the public domain has to see budgeting as a political choice involving the definition of need and the allocation of resources to competing needs. Stewart and Ranson argue that accountability is both wider and deeper in the public sector, with a greater number of key groups of people to whom to account, including politicians (local and national), general public, service users and ministers. In the private sector accountability can be defined in a single dimension: shareholders.

At the opposite extreme, authors such as Murray (1975) suggest that public and private management are converging. Murray argues, albeit from an American perspective, that management can be 'viewed as a generic process, with universal implications and with application in any institutional setting, whether a private firm or public agency'.[6]

Other academics fall between the differentialist and genericist schools of thought. Rainey et al for example, conceived of the

4. For a more detailed discussion of the factors see SPARKS et al, (1996), op cit, pp299-302.

5. J STEWART and S RANSON (1988) Management in the Public Domain, Journal of Public Money and Management April-June 1996, pp5-7.

6. N MURRAY (1975) comparing Public and Private Management: An Exploratory Essay, Public Administration Review, Vol 35, No. 4.

'publicness' of an organisation as a question of degree, something that depended on the extent to which a set of attributes was present or absent.[7] The management of core public sector organisations requires different competencies and skills from the management of core private sector organisations. The management of all non-core organisations requires similar skills according to Rainey. Rainey's is a substantive piece of work as it is based on a survey of literature, including a number of empirical studies. It is clear that Stewart and Ranson had in mind what Rainey would term a hard core public organisation, rather than a borderline public/private one, which may explain their more sweeping differentialist claims. The debate has recently taken one step forward with a development in the public sector operating environment.

New Public Management

The election of a Conservative government in 1979, which was committed to a manifesto which promised to reduce public expenditure and the role of the state by reducing waste and bureaucracy, resulted in a major reform programme which affected the Prison Service, like other central government departments. Thatcherism included a clear political commitment to reducing the size of the Civil Service and to increasing the efficiency of government. This was to be achieved by altering the cultural attitudes and behaviour of civil servants and by radical structural reform. The cultural shift which began in the 1980s was a clear attempt to move from an administrative to a managerial culture. The creation of an Efficiency Strategy, under the guidance of Sir Derek Rayner, led to a series of scrutinies within individual departments aimed at identifying and eliminating areas of waste, inefficiency, duplication and overlap.

As Metcalfe and Richards point out, in their work on improving public management, the long term goal was lasting reforms of structures, systems, personnel policies, and deeply ingrained attitudes and beliefs.[8]

7. H RAINEY, R BACKOFF, C LEVINE (1976) Comparing Public and Private Organisations, Public Administration Review, Vol 36..

8. L METCALFE and S RICHARDS (1990) Improving Public Management, Second Edn: Sage.

The Ibbs Report on Improving Management in Government, published in 1988, marked a further move in the managerialisation of government. The Report recommended three main priorities:

- the work of each department must be organised in a way which focuses on the job to be done; the systems and structures must enhance the effective delivery of policies and services;
- the management of each department must ensure that staff have the relevant experience and skills needed to do the tasks that are essential to effective government;
- there must be a real and sustained pressure on and within each department for continuous improvement in the value for money obtained in the delivery of policies and services.[9]

In order to focus on the job to be done, the report recommended the creation of agencies to carry out the executive functions of government within a policy and resources framework set by a department.

As a result of this political pressure for change, the 1980s witnessed the importation of a number of management techniques new to the public sector. It has been argued that behind these surface manifestations of change lay the rise of new sets of key managerial ideas, beliefs and behaviours. These ideas and beliefs grouped together have become known as New Public Management (NPM).[10] The strategy behind NPM consists of three elements: cash limits and emphasis on efficiency to engender a more financially aware and prudent approach; greater standardisation in policies and practices to curb the autonomy of the professionals and reduce their idiosyncrasies; and reorganisation into stronger hierarchies, supported by target setting and performance monitoring to effect greater control and to sharpen accountability.

Considered holistically, NPM represents a major attempt to restructure public services, changing the nature of their organisation and management. Research suggests that these reform programmes contain multiple strands which impact at system, group and individual role levels alike. Whilst the general pressure for change is constant, the rate and pace of change has varied from one organisation to another.

9. R IBBS (1988) Improving Management in Government: The Next Steps, London: HMSO.

10. A useful summary of the rise of New Public Management in E FERLIE, A PETTIGREW, L ASHBURNER and L FITZGERALD (1996). The New Public Management in Action, Oxford: Oxford University Press.

The impact of NPM on the institutions responsible for criminal justice has been analysed by Raine and Willson who found that:

> 'To differing degrees, the organisational culture and ways of working of the criminal justice agencies, like all other public sector organisations, have been transformed in recent years by the wave of managerialism in part promoted and imposed by 'new right' politicians as they have sought to inject private sector principles and practices into the public sector, but which have also come to be seen as having a status and significance above party policies: as a global phenomenon of our time.'[11]

The arrival in criminal justice of managerialism was, according to Raine and Willson, somewhat slower than in most other parts of the UK public service, notably local and central government. In their view this was as a result of the high political priority afforded to law and order by the new Conservative government in 1979 and partly because of the cultural segregation and organisational positioning of the criminal justice agencies. However, as Lacey points out, most of the criminal justice initiatives which the government took from the mid 1980s onwards appear to contain, or were founded upon, elements of the public sector managerialist agenda.[12]

The then Prison Department, like other government departments, introduced a seminal document which marked its implementation of the managerialist agenda. In the case of the Prison Department, Circular Instruction 55 of 1984 defined the management accountabilities within the Service. The main principles were:

- the key manager was the prison governor and was charged with the delivery of the Department's policy and was responsible for the staff of the institution;
- the framework for the policy was set out as the task of the Prison Service and a broad statement of the functions of the establishments; and

11. J RAINE and M WILLSON (1997) Beyond Managerialism in Criminal Justice, The Howard Journal, Vol 36, No 1, February 1997, pp 80-95 Blackwell Publishers.

12. N LACEY (1994) Government as Manager, Citizen as Consumer: The Case of the Criminal Justice Act 1991: Modern Law Review 75, pp 534-554.

- ✦ the governor's accountability was defined by explicit terms of reference agreed with the line manager and accounted for formally in an annual report.

Figure 6 : Doctrinal Components of New Public Management (adapted from Hood 1991)

No.	Doctrine	Meaning	Prison Service Impact
1	Hands-on professional . management in the public sector as Director General.	Active visible control of organisations from named persons at the top tree to manage.	Recruitment of Directors from private sector (Lewis as Director General; Landers as Director of Finance, and Scott as Director of Personnel).
2	Explicit standards and measures of performance..	Definition of goals, targets, indicators of success, preferably expressed in quantitative terms.	Key Performance Indicators and Goals set out in the Prison Service Corporate Plan and in contracts for each prison.
3	Greater emphasis on output controls.	Resource allocation and rewards linked to measured performance; break-up of centralised bureaucracy-wide personnel management.	Devolution of Personnel/Finance to governors.
4	Shift to desegregation of units in the public sector.	Break-up of formerly 'monolithic' structures into corporate units around geography or products, operating on decentralised 'one-line' budgets and dealing with one another on an 'arms-length' basis.	Creation of Headquarters Groups, Central Service Units and Areas.
5	Shift to greater competition in public sector.	Move to term contracts and public tendering procedures.	Contracting out prisons and escorts. Service Level Agreements for example, HMP Manchester.
6	Stress on private sector styles of management practice.	Move away from military-style 'public service ethic' greater flexibility in hiring and rewards; greater use of	Introduction of Performance Pay.

		performance related techniques.	
7	Stress on greater discipline and parsimony in resource use. limiting 'compliance costs'	Cutting direct costs, raising labour discipline, resisting union demands, to business.	Trade Union reform through Criminal Justice and Public Order Act. Reduced Budgets.

The publication of CI 55/1984 signalled the start of two years' work of translating the 22 proposed functions into specific terms for each establishment. When coupled with developments in working procedures, a statement of available resources, and an annual assignment of priorities for the governor, the 'functions document' gradually moved towards the start of a contract between the governor and his or her line manager.[13]

Other aspects of NPM were slowly introduced during the late 1980s and early 1990s. The full impact of NPM on the Prison Service can be seen in figure 6 which adopts Hood's seven doctrinal components of NPM.[14] Hood found that different commentators and advocates of NPM stressed varying aspects of doctrine but that several overlapping precepts existed.

NPM has therefore become firmly entrenched within the Prison Service with its emphasis on productivity, cost efficiency, league tables of performance statistics and contracting out. Some aspects of NPM, such as devolution of personnel matters, budgets and improved financial accountability, have generally been welcomed by governors. Other aspects, including contracting out, reduced budgets and the creation of quantitative key performance indicators have not been greeted with universal approval. For some governors the managerialist culture does not fit readily with their caring and reforming ideals, as it has attempted significantly to change their orientation, value base and ways of working. The language and tools of managerialism (for example, managing director instead of governor, strategic and business

13. For a detailed review of the management changes in the Prison Service during the 1980s see R EVANS (1990) Management Models and Performance Monitoring in the Prison Department, Prison Service Journal, No 78, Spring 1990, pp 2-9. A copy of CI55/84 together with the rationale for its introduction can be found in J REYNOLDS and U SMARTT (1996) Prison Policy and Practice, Prison Service Journal, pp152-159.

14. C HOOD (1991) A Public Management for all Seasons, Public Administration, Vol 69, Spring 1991, pp 3-19.

plans, units as a term for prisoners) have been criticised as being inappropriate for use in a caring profession.[15]

Indeed, the main thrust of attempts to recapture the 'public management variable' are based on the belief that public bodies ought to achieve their ends by embodying certain values and that it is the 'values' element which differentiates the 'value-free' and 'ethically neutral' private sector.[16]

The reality of NPM has made the governor focus more on performance indicators, measures, business planning and budgets than ever before. The main result of this has been a reduction in the direct management of prisoners by governors. Governors have been forced to limit the amount of time they spend conducting adjudications, hearing applications and touring the prison. The days of the 'hands on' governor who knew the names of all their prisoners and staff are long gone (if they ever existed). As early as 1994 governors were expressing concern about the new approach to governing. Michael Selby, in an article written shortly after his retirement as a governor, summed up the feeling at the time:

> 'All governors are certain that the style of governing will have to change. More and more, governors will be office bound. As one governor put it: 'it is not my job to care for prisoners but to care for staff who care for prisoners'. Governors must learn to delegate to survive, but the result is that they will be much less in evidence and certainly less accessible. Will this mean that the special skills that were traditionally required for successful governing are no longer required?'[17]

The 'competent' governor

The advance of NPM has helped to blur the distinction between public and private competence. If one accepts the definition of competence as the set of behaviour patterns that an incumbent needs to bring to a position in order to perform their tasks and functions

15. D WILSON (1995) Against the Culture of Management, Prison Service Journal No. 98, March 1995, pp 7-9.

16. For an exploratory essay on the subject see J DiIULIO (1989) Recovering the Public Management Variable: Lessons from Schools, Prisons and Armies, Public Administration Review, Vol 49, March/April, p127-133.

17. M SELBY (1994) Goals for Gaolers?, Prison Report No 98, Autumn, pp 22-23.

effectively, then senior management competence may be similar in public and private sectors.[18] Authors such as Boyatzis attempt to identify a set of generic managerial competence that are indicative of superior organisational performance and are interchangeable throughout a variety of seemingly different organisations.[19]

The Prison Service, when it became an Agency , was encouraged, like other executive agencies, to consider developing a competence framework. Following protracted discussions and research the Prisons Board rejected generic models of managerial competence in favour of an organisation specific model which was more behaviour based and expressive of the language, culture and environment of the Service. The core competence framework (CCF) for the Prison Service was accepted in late 1996. The CCF was intended to inform the recruitment, selection and development processes of staff and was to be integrated and designed to assist the delivery of other Prison Service strategic processes. Unlike the Home Office, the Prison Service CCF does not have competencies identified for each managerial level but rather is a framework of 12 competencies applicable to all staff in the Service. Each of the 12 competencies has three over arching sentences attached to describe and a number of performance indicators.[20]

A comparison of the Prison Service CCF with a survey of 74 competence frameworks in both private and public sector organisations indicates a degree of similarity.[21] Figure 7 below shows the Prison Service CCF and the competencies identified most frequently by the 74 organisations. The survey sample included 32 per cent public sector organisations but no indication is given in the research data as to whether the type of competence was public or private sector specific.

18. See R BOAM and P SPARROW (1992) Designing and Achieving Competency: McGraw-Hill.

19. R BOYATZIS (1982) The Competent Manager, A Model for Effective Performance, New York: Wylie and Sons.

20. A copy of the Prison Service Core Competency Framework is contained in Appendix 2.

21. The survey was conducted by Industrial Relations Services and published as annual Survey of Competency Frameworks in Competency, Vol 4, No 1, Autumn 1996.

Figure 7 : Comparison of Core Competencies

Prison Service Core Competence Framework	IRS (1996) Survey, 14 most frequently identified managerial competencies
Security awareness	Communication
Concern for prisoner care	Results orientated
Rehabilitation orientated	Customer focus
Systematic approach	Teamwork
Planning and renewing	Leadership
Organising and empowering	Planning and organising
Team playing and networking	Business awareness
Team building and liaison	Flexibility/adaptability
Motivation and commitment	Developing others
Communicates clearly	Problem solving
Problem solving and continuous improvement	Analytical thinking
Leadership and decision making	Building relationships
	Decision making
	Influencing/facilitating

The Prison Service CCF contains three organisation specific competencies (security awareness, concern for prisoner care, and rehabilitation orientated). These were included to reinforce the Prison Service Purpose, Vision, Goals and Values, (which were later replaced by Objectives and Principles). The remaining nine competencies are applicable to both the public and private sectors. The Prison Service CCF does not include customer focus and commercial business awareness, which were high in the IRS survey list, perhaps because these are more private sector/service sector orientated competencies.

For any individual to be competent to do a job not only requires behaviour competencies but underpinning knowledge and skills. Again, the senior management knowledge and skills required in both the public and private sectors are now similar. The Management Charter Initiative (MCI) has identified generic Senior Management Standards, which are grouped under four headings:

- understanding and influencing the environment;
- setting the strategy and gaining commitment;
- planning and implementing; and
- monitoring, evaluating and improving performance.

Clearly, prison governors are required to undertake these managerial tasks and functions. Business planning, reviewing performance, monitoring, strategic planning, and introducing and managing change is as necessary for governors as for chief executives or managing directors in the private sector.

If effective, prison governors share the same behavioural and managerial competencies as successful senior managers in the private sector, but why then is governing sui generis? One element is the moral dimension to the job of running prisons. The various moral standpoints of governors are discussed in the next section.

Operating credos

Rutherford, in his discussions with 28 senior criminal justice practitioners (including Prison Service personnel), found three dominant ideologies or credos existed: the punishment credo; the efficiency credo and the humanity credo.[22] None of the practitioners articulated a precisely formulated working ideology, rather the working credo emerged during their interviews. This supports earlier research which found that credos tend to be preconscious rather than explicitly held.[23] The relationship between values and a person's work was found to be a dynamic and developmental process, as one would expect. Personal maturity, professional experience, and the broader social and political content all impact on an individual's working credo.

The punishment credo was associated with a powerfully held dislike, and moral condemnation of, offenders. Proponents of this credo argue that, once caught, offenders should be dealt with in ways that were punitive and degrading. As such this is very much a punitive-retaliatory approach to criminal justice. The humanity credo however has empathy with offenders at its core. The credo embraces an optimism that constructive work can be done; an adherence to the rule of law; and an insistence upon open and accountable procedures. Such a credo is firmly established within the liberal humane and sociological approach. The efficiency credo has its base firmly in an expedient managerialist approach, eschewing any claim to a moral mission and favouring smooth management. The orientation of followers of this credo is towards institutionally defined managerial goals.

22. A RUTHERFORD (1993) Criminal Justice and the Pursuit of Decency: Oxford University Press. See also A RUTHERFORD (1993) Penal Policy and Prison Management, Prison Service Journal No 90, pp 26-29.

23. W MILLER (1973) Ideology and Criminal Justice Policy: Some Current Issues, Journal of Criminal Law and Criminology No 64, pp 142-162.

The ascendancy of NPM has brought with it a growth in the efficiency credo. Advocates of the humanity credo have found their values increasingly challenged by the advocates of both the efficiency and the punishment credos. An increasing number of governors are being pressurised to adopt an approach which is based on the efficiency credo. A similar situation developed in the USA. Jacobs provides a good example of the operation of the efficiency credo in the form of the new warden of Stateville Prison, Illinois.

> 'The incoming warden brought to the prison a commitment to scientific management rather than any correctional ideology ... (he) is neither in favour nor opposed to rehabilitative programmes. His primary commitment is to running a safe, clean, programme-orientated institution which functions smoothly on a day-to-day basis and that is not in violation of code provisions, administrative regulations or court orders. He has brought a new definition of administration to the prison. He stresses efficiency and emotionally detached management. He has attempted to remove the affect attached to handling inmates.'[24]

Rutherford argues that the preoccupation with expedient managerialism has resulted in a move from concern for prisoners to narrowly defined performance measures and to short term troubleshooting. He quotes a number of governors in support of this position. More recently, Godfrey outlined the concerns of many governors about the rise of managerialism and the demise of the rehabilitative ideal:

> 'Values and policies to which governors have long been committed are now derided as soft-headed and soft-hearted ... One consequence of the trend towards pragmatism is that we have become accustomed to seeing efficiency as the only goal ... to the extent that most of us still dare to think about issues of principle. I believe that one of the reasons for governors' depression is that many of us do not share the values underlying current policies. Nor do we believe that those

24. J JACOBS (1997) Stateville: The Penitentiary in Mass Society, Chicago: University of Chicago Press pp 103-104.

policies are in the best interests of victims, potential victims, offenders or their families'.[25]

Whilst Godfrey does not speak for all governors his assertions would support Rutherford's view that the efficiency credo is in the ascendancy, even though for many governors it seems to conflict with the humanity credo. Sparks, Bottoms and Hay, in their book on prisons and the problem of order, note that the new managerialism in the Prison Service is seen by its critics as eroding the traditional moral (including reformative) commitments of institutions in favour of an exclusive concern with process and measurement.[26]

Models of prison management

It is generally agreed that there is a direct connection between what governors believe and value, and how their prisons are run. DiIulio noted that 'seemingly slight philosophical differences give rise to marked differences in correctional policies, practices and procedures'.[27] The differing beliefs, values and credos identified by Rutherford should, according to DiIulio, influence the individual's management philosophy and style, and by extension the operation of the prison.

Barak-Glantz, who did the pioneering work in prison management approaches, identified four models of prison management: authoritarian model; bureaucratic lawful model; shared-powers model and inmate control model.[28] The models are described in the form of Weberian 'ideal types' and Barak-Glantz recognises that few prisons can be classed as entirely one or another of the models. What distinguishes one style from another is the predominance of certain central characteristics of a particular model.

The chief characteristic of the authoritarian model is the domination of the governor over staff as well as prisoners. The governor exercises complete power with few restraints on its arbitrary use. In this model governors tend to have remained in post for a very long period and view the prison as a 'totalitarian island' in which they

25. D GODFREY (1996) The Morale of Prison Govenors: Some Reflections, Prison Service Journal March 1996, No 104, p12-14.

26. R SPARKS, A BOTTOMS, W HAY (1996) Prisons and the Problem of Order, Oxford: Clarendon Press.

27. J DiIULIO (1987) Governing Prisons: A Comparative Study of Correctional Management, New York: Freedom Press, p165.

28. I BARAK-GLANTZ (1981) Towards a Conceptual Scheme of Prison Management, Prison Service Journal, Vol 61, Part 2, pp 42-60.

can do as they please, so long as they stay within the extremely broad limits of their authority.

In his description of the 'authoritarian prison' McCleery describes the operation of this model: 'A high degree of discipline was maintained with a minimum of direct sanctions. Control, rather than 'justice' in the familiar sense was the object.'[29] The authoritarian model can lead, it is argued, to abuses of power, authority and privilege. The single ruler, whether benevolent or despotic, and the associated authoritarian administrative style, has largely disappeared, even though some would argue that some prison fiefdoms, reminiscent of a medieval barony, still exist.

The bureaucratic-lawful model is often implemented as a reaction to the authoritarian model. In the bureaucratic-lawful model general principles, rules and regulations are applied by the central administration to the governor, and by the governor to his or her staff. Vagg argues that this makes the governor 'simply one link in a bureaucratic chain'.[30] In addition to the proliferation of instructions and orders cascading from above, the bureaucratic-lawful model often involves pressure to run the prison like a private corporation and to ensure a cost effective operation. As a result, professional accountants and administrators are brought into the prison to assist the governor, who increasingly becomes a desk bound manager. The prison is seen as any other bureaucracy and the governor a 'prison manager' or 'prison bureaucrat'.

The third model, the shared-powers model, refers to a situation in which rehabilitative goals led to the democratisation of the prison, with some power being given to prisoners, who form identifiable pressure groups. This model is characterised by a rehabilitative and democratic ideology, the recognition of legitimate rights and of conflict between uniformed grades and governor grades. Treatment-orientated governors believe that only the minimum and absolutely necessary levels of control be maintained in order to facilitate reform and rehabilitation and that a democratic prison system is necessary to achieve the reform. It is argued that the push for democratisation (in the name of therapy) creates a power vacuum to which prisoners, as well as staff, respond by attempting to advance their respective interests. Groups of prisoners, such as lifers, prisoners on therapy, or ethnic

29. T McCLEERY (1996) 'Policy Change in Prison Management' in A ETZIONE (ed) Complex Organisations: A Sociological Reader, New York; Holt Rinehort and Winston.

30. J VAGG (1994) Prison Systems - A Comparative Study of Accountability in England, France, Germany and the Netherlands, Oxford: Clarendon Press, p11.

minorities, form to advance common interests and to speak with a single voice. In more extreme cases militant prisoners' rights groups or unions form to push for perceived rights. Staff groups feel under threat and respond by making more extreme demands. The formation of prisoner groups and committees often antagonise uniformed staff who perceive it as a loss of power and authority. Attempts to introduce reform and rehabilitation can, in the shared-powers model, result in a clash of conflicting interests.

The inmate-control model involves prisoner groups, perhaps based on sub-cultures outside of prison, taking control of the prison by creating no-go areas, organising activities and settling disputes amongst themselves. Although contained within the perimeter of the wing or prison, the prisoners exercise real control and their leaders create rules, monitor behaviour and punish transgressors with relative impunity. Prisoners divide into religious, ethnic or 'street gang' groups within a relatively well organised structure, clear leadership and a chain of command. Their actions and behaviours often support deviant behaviour as a means to gain further power, by, for example, establishing and controlling no-go areas; allocating wing jobs and cell allocation and punishing vulnerable prisoners (such as sex offenders) located on a normal wing.

It is perhaps difficult to identify a prison which equates exactly with each type of model in this country. However, it is possible to identify in the United States and some eastern European countries more extreme examples of each model. DiIulio, for example, describes the prison systems in three American states: Texas, Michigan and California.[31]

The Texas system is described as operating a 'control' model (similar to Barak-Glantz's authoritarian model) where emphasis is placed on prisoner obedience, work and education, set within a paramilitary style of organisation. The Michigan system is a 'responsibility' model (roughly equivalent to Barak-Glantz's shared-power model) in which the focus is more on classification and grievance procedures and, subject to security issues, prisoners are given some responsibility for their own daily lives. Control is maintained where possible through consultations rather than orders. The third state, California, is described as a 'consensual model' (somewhere between the authoritarian and shared power models of Barak-Glantz). The

31. DiIULIO (1987), op cit.

consensual model is a combination of both control and responsibility styles, with paramilitary staff who deal with prisoners informally where possible and with extensive grievance procedures.

Prison leadership

The role of the governor as leader was briefly outlined in Chapter 2. However, reaching a consensus about the nature of leadership has proved elusive over the years. Leadership constantly runs the risk of being all things to all people; a nebulous catch-all phrase. Indeed, it can be argued that leadership is constantly in a state of evolution and flux so that its essence can never be captured.

However, many of the reports about the Prison Service, in the wake of escapes, riots or industrial relations problems, have suggested that if leadership had been demonstrated by managers then the problem would not have occurred in the first place. The Learmont Report, for example, made clear that 'positive and visible leadership which recognises the human dimensions, shows enthusiasm for people's efforts and promotes feelings of self respect and self confidence' would overcome the problem of staff intimidations, manipulations and boredom (recommendation 99).[32] More recently the Prison Service Review noted the 'requirement for a particularly high level of managerial and leadership skill in the Prison Service' (paragraph 9.4) and commended the Service to devise a 'leadership charter' which would be an expression of the desired organisational culture (paragraph 3.29).[33]

The importance of various elements within leadership were reinforced by the new Director General of the Prison Service, Martin Narey, shortly after he took up post.[34] In an Eve Saville Memorial lecture Narey made clear that:

> 'Leadership in the Prison Service requires personal and moral courage. This is not a job that can or should be done in a detached or neutral way. There is an inescapable moral dimension to the Service's work. Those of us who aspire to lead within it have to know what we believe to be right and to

32. Review of Prison Service Security in England and Wales and the escape from Parkhurst Prison on Tuesday 3rd January 1995 (Learmont Report) (1995). Cmnd 3020; HMSO. London.

33. HM Prison Service (1997) Prison Service Review.

34. M NAREY (1999) Taking the Prison Service into the 21st Century, Criminal Justice Matters No 36 pp29-309.

trust that instinct both in moments of crisis and in charting a strategy for the future'.

Few organisations take leadership seriously enough to articulate its role in the organisation and their views on what makes for good leadership. The few organisations that have done so have drawn up a leadership charter. The Prison Service Review recommended that the Prison Service do the same and draw up a leadership charter for the Prison Service. Using the Prison Service Core Competency Framework, the evolving model of leadership and other leadership charters, an attempt was made to articulate a leadership charter for the Prison Service in 1998.[35]

Prison Service Leadership Charter

Prison Service Leadership Charter identifies the behaviour which the Prison Service believes is vital to achieve its Purpose, Vision, Goals and Values.

Vision

A leader:

- ✦ Provides a clear personal vision which aligns with the Prison Service Purpose, Vision, Goals and Values and captures the imagination.
- ✦ Describes the vision in simple language and frequently checks understanding.
- ✦ Translates the vision into measurable goals that stretch the leader and the team.

Commitment

A leader:

- ✦ Takes ownership of ideas adopted by the Service whatever the prior debate.
- ✦ Demonstrates consistent and constant personal commitment to the vision through appropriate allocation of resources and the use of personal time.
- ✦ Secures the personal commitment of immediate colleagues.

35. S BRYANS and J WALFORD (1998) Leadership in the Prison Service. Prison Service Journal No 119, pp 10-13.

- Places emphasis on gaining enthusiastic acceptance as well as directing the process of change.

Approach

A leader creates the desired Prison Service culture by emphasising behaviours under the following headings:

1 People

A leader places emphasis on:

Encouraging open and honest communication with individuals and teams.

- Coaching staff and gives opportunity for self development learning.
- Team goals and priorities.
- Commitment to equality of opportunity.
- Realistic personal objectives and priorities.
- Recognising the potential in others.
- Adopting different leadership styles and using them effectively as required.
- Ensuring staff have a safe and secure working environment.
- Giving praise and recognition where appropriate.
- Demonstrating support and care for colleagues.
- Creating an atmosphere of honesty, trust and mutual support.

2. Organisational Performance

A leader places emphasis on:

- Analysing situations in terms of deliverables and output and look for continuous improvement.
- Reviewing and monitoring priorities against agreed objectives.
- Encouraging a pro active approach where appropriate.
- Systematically collecting and appraising information.
- Working within budgetary constraints.
- Using fact and judgement to take decisions at an appropriate level.
- Setting high minimum standards.
- Continuous performance improvements.
- Flexibility in meeting changing demands.

3. Personal Contribution

A leader places emphasis on:

- ✦ Upholding Prison Service Values.
- ✦ Displaying high personal levels of competence and judgement, caring and integrity.
- ✦ Accepting personal accountability.
- ✦ Being self assured, decisive and creating a good impression.
- ✦ Inspiring confidence.
- ✦ Being self disciplined, loyal and ready to accept responsibility.
- ✦ Being highly motivated to achieve.
- ✦ Learning from mistakes made.
- ✦ Being accessible and visible.
- ✦ Seeking input and listening carefully.
- ✦ Developing and maintaining a team.
- ✦ Showing humility.

Communication

A leader:

- ✦ Identifies the communication implications of every policy, decision and situation.
- ✦ Plans the communication activity including the definition, consistency, regularity and timing of the key messages.
- ✦ Uses a range of channels while placing a particular emphasis on face to face: is open, honest and positive.
- ✦ Seeks input and listens carefully.
- ✦ Uses measurements to ensure the consistency and effectiveness of the communication process.

The reality of governing

The Prison Service Review made clear that it thought 'Prisons remain very hierarchical and almost feudal. There is a strong dependency on the role and person of the governor. Research has shown that a well run prison runs more than anything else on the skill and approach of the governor. The key managerial role in the Prison Service is that of the governor.'[36] Despite the acceptance of the importance of governors the Chief Inspector of Prisons commented that:

36. HM Prison Service (1997) op cit, para 9.14 and 10.9.

> 'I am appalled at the bureaucratic load that is devolved down to governors, requiring them to complete a plethora of short notice reports and returns, as well as assimilate the mountain of Instructions. My concern arises from the number of times that governors complain to me about the effect that all this had on the amount of time they can spend walking their prisons. This goes back to my contention that governing governors must be helped to govern their prisons and exercise leadership of their staff. To bog them down in bureaucratic detail shows a lack of awareness of the load on governors, and the fact that inhibiting their ability to walk their prisons is bound to have an effect on the operational performance of staff, which in turn affects the delivery of the operational aim.'[37]

The reality of governing is that the governor must cope with a myriad of pressures and competing demands. He or she must, at the same time, be an effective general manager, have public sector competence, be able to command incidents and demonstrate the 'sui generis' element of governing - prison management ability. Each of these four elements is explored at some length in an article in the Howard Journal.[38] A brief summary from the article of the last three competence areas is given below. The fourth, general management competence, has already been covered earlier in this chapter.

Public sector management competence

The governor, as a manager in the public sector, requires public sector management competence in addition to general manager competence. All senior public sector employees require knowledge of government and of the principles according to which it functions. In particular, an understanding of three guiding doctrines of the constitution: sovereignty or supremacy of Parliament, ministerial responsibility; and the rule of law.

Private sector management does not contain a close equivalent to the role of politicians in public sector management. Governors require clear insight into the essentially political dimension of all public sector working. When the Prison Service became an Agency in 1993, there was

37. Annual Report of HM Chief Inspector of Prisons 1997-1998 (1999) HMSO: London.

38. S BRYANS (2000) 'Governing Prisons: An Analysis of who is Governing Prisons and the Competencies which they require to govern effectively.' The Howard Journal, Vol 30, No 1, Feb 2000, pp 14-29.

a widespread misconception among governors about its effect. Many believed that the Prison Service would have the independence they felt it wanted and deserved - independence from the main Home Office and ministers. The reality is that 'it is inevitable that ministers will be interested in and wish to influence the executive functions of the Prison Service, (for example): its operations'.[39] The Home Secretary has a legitimate interest in the operational performance of the Prison Service, not least as he will be called into account in Parliament for it. The accountability of ministers for the actions of officials was made quite clear by Lord Greene:

> 'The duties imposed upon Ministers and the powers given to Ministers are normally exercised under the authority of Ministers by responsible officials of the department ... Constitutionally, the decisions of such an official is of course, the decision of the Minister, the Minister is responsible. It is he who must answer before Parliament for anything his officials have done under authority.'[40]

The present administration announced on 15 May 1997 that, in future, all Parliamentary Questions about the Prison Service would be answered by a Home Office minister and not by the Director General or another senior Prison Service official. A subsequent statement made clear that this change 'will enable ministers to answer personally to Parliament for what is done in our prisons'.[41] Members of Parliament have been encouraged to write directly to the Director General or, where they see fit, to governors of individual establishments concerning matters raised by individual constituents on delegated matters. However, if they are not content with the reply, they can take the matter up with ministers in writing or by way of a Parliamentary Question. Governors must, therefore, take great care in preparing material for headquarters and MPs to ensure that the information contained therein is accurate and not misleading. In addition, governors need to ensure that the material does not display a lack of political awareness or fails to take into account relevant policy issues.

39. Prison Service Review, op cit p34.
40. Carltona v Works Commission (1943) All ER 560.
41. Hansard, 31 July 1997, written answers 91.

Governors need to develop an awareness that all their actions need to be judged against whether they fit with ministers' policies and, where there is doubt, to seek advice from more senior staff. The ability to know when an issue has a policy, political or tactical element is critical. A good example of where this did not take place was the proposal by a governor to build a pitch and putt course in their prison.[42] The Home Secretary did not consider that it had a place in his 'decent but austere' prison regimes and had the decision overturned after much embarrassment to the Prison Service and ministers. Governors must ensure that they avoid taking steps which might result in political comment or criticism of the minister. To be a competent governor, therefore, individuals must understand the rules and conventions within which they operate. In this particular context, that requires a knowledge and understanding of the political framework and the pattern of current political debate concerning criminal justice. Governors need also to be aware of three mechanisms which are used to scrutinise the activity of civil servants in relation to prisons: The Prisons Ombudsman; the use of select committees, in particular the Home Affairs Select Committee, and the National Audit Office.

Governors and, indeed, all public sector managers, have to act within the law. That does not make them different from managers in the private sector. The general principle of abiding by the law applies to all and, at least as a starting point, the public sector manager is equally subject to private law as are private sector managers. Yet, additionally, there is a body of public law applying to public sector managers. The administration of a sentence of imprisonment involves the exercise of public power. Richardson makes clear that 'in both prison and secure hospitals, extensive areas of discretion are granted to the relevant authorities, who are empowered to intervene most directly in the lives and liberties of individuals'.[43] As officials, governors may have power, but they have to act within the law. Administrative action by the governor is subject to judicial review if it is illegal, unreasonable or if procedural impropriety has taken place. Whilst the intricacies of administrative law are matters for lawyers, the level of awareness expected of officials means that governors must be alert to the tests

42. D LEWIS (1997) Hidden Agendas: Politics, Law and Disorder. Hamish Hamilton: London p63.

43. G RICHARDSON (1993) Law, Process and Custody: Prisoners and Patients. Weidenfield and Nicholson, London, p1.

under each of these categories that the courts may use for reviewing their decisions and the decisions for which they are responsible. This involves governors knowing what the law allows them to do; recognising the difference between a duty and a power; ensuring jurisdiction, unfettered discretion and rightful delegation; understanding when an action would be held to be irrational or unreasonable; using powers for only 'proper' purposes; avoiding procedural illegality and ensuring that their actions are not contrary to the common law rules of natural justice by ensuring bias is avoided and fairness is maintained. Chapter 7 outlines a number of cases where a governor's decision has been challenged in the courts.

Public sector managers tend to have less clarity in terms of the objectives for their organisations than private sector managers. The objectives, goals and performance criteria of public sector services tend to be multiple and diverse, vague and intangible and often conflicting.[44] This is certainly true of the Prison Service and recent commentators have made the point that there is 'widespread confusion over the present Statement of Purpose of the Service. The two objectives (custody and care) provide a constant and inevitable tension'.[45] Public sector organisations have multiple stakeholder groups. Managers in the public sector are pushed and pulled within this network of stakeholders. The latter are fairly unlikely to hold identical views of what the desirable priorities are, the allocation of resources or even sometimes what the basic mission should be. Prisons clearly do not exist in a vacuum and the Prison Service's myriad of stakeholders include: prisoners' families; general public; pressure groups; politicians; media; staff; Home Office and local communities. Governors need to understand that their decisions are value laden. It has been pointed out elsewhere that 'managers in the public sector have to be sensitive to the values inherent in its actions'.[46] Public sector managers must be able to balance the competing demands and values in order to achieve an effective outcome. Few private sector managers have quite so many stakeholders to satisfy. Public sector managers have, therefore, to manage dissatisfaction to a much greater extent. Dissatisfaction may be caused by the allocation of resources or services, the quality of that

---

44. R RAINEY, R BACKOFF and C LEVINE (1976) 'Comparing Public and Private Organisations', Public Administration Review Vol 36.

45. Review of Prison Service Security (Learmont Report) (1995) Cmnd 3020 HMSO: London.

46. J STEWART and S RANSON (1995) 'Management in the Public Domain in: D MCKEVITT and A LAWTON, Public Sector Management: Sage: London.

service or by legal constraints placed upon the public sector manager in the exercising of their powers. Governors, in particular, need to be competent at managing dissatisfaction as seldom a day passes without the governor having to make an unpopular decision, either with reference to staff or in relation to prisoners.

Incident command competence

Freeman rightly points out that the 'ultimate goal of all correctional administrators is to manage a facility or agency in such a way that emergencies are prevented. However, despite our best efforts, there are times when we cannot control the actions of others'.[47] Governors need to be able to respond to a range of possible incidents which can occur in their prisons. Incidents such as fires, riots, demonstrations, escapes, hostages, bombs, roof top protests and gang fights can occur spontaneously with little, if any, warning. Command differs from management and effective managers may not be able to act successfully in a command role. The requirement to act in a command role is not, however, unique to the prison governor. A range of individuals may have to act as the key decision maker in a crisis, including: members of the fire, ambulance, police and coastguard services; airline pilots; military officers and duty managers of off-shore oil wells, industrial plants, entertainment venues, hotels and other public buildings.

The notion that 'command' differs from 'management' is now widely accepted. The difference between command in an emergency and routine management has been highlighted in the following way: 'Command is predominantly subjective and directive. Management is predominantly objective and consultative. An important subsidiary conclusion is that the application of conventional management techniques can ironically be quite dangerous in an emergency'.[48] More recently, Murray highlighted other aspects of the distinctiveness of the command role: 'Commanding critical resources when life, property and the environment are at risk is a very unique and demanding situation. The exercise of command at an operational incident is complex. Incident commanders must realise the responsibilities faced, recognise

47. R FREEMAN (1996) Strategic planning for correctional emergencies: ACA, Lanham, MDF.

48. J LARKEN (1992) The Command requirement and OIM qualification quoted in R FLIN (1996) Sitting in the hot seat - leaders and teams for critical incident management. Chichester: Wiley and Sons..

authority possessed, assess the situation, make decisions and take action which meets the expectations of all those who serve'.[49]

The complexity of commanding incidents, which are often characterised by ambiguous and conflicting information, shifting goals, time pressure, dynamic conditions, complex operational team structures and poor communication, is often ignored. Successful incident command is seldom acknowledged or recognised and it is only where command goes wrong that the media take an interest. Examples are the Piper Alpha platform disaster, the Hillsborough stadium disaster and Kings Cross underground fire. In the prison context, the Woolf Inquiry , which looked into the riots at HMP Manchester and elsewhere in April 1990, found that the reason why the disturbance developed so rapidly was due to the 'inept handling at the early stages of the disturbance' and the commanders' inability to provide the necessary leadership and control during the initial period of the disturbance.[50]

Research indicates that successful incident commanders tend to have certain attributes, which can be expressed in terms of personality traits, and certain command skills.[51] Whilst many of these individual traits and skills are required in general management, commanding an incident requires a directive and a less democratic style of leadership. Good commanders will still solicit advice from available experts and listen to more junior staff, but act in a more authoritarian form due to the high time pressure and risks involved in incidents. As Flin points out, 'the need for a perceptible change in leadership style ... sends a very important message to the rest of the team that the situation is serious and that they will have to 'change gear' and sharpen their performance'.[52] Some organisations have gone so far as to produce occupational standards for incident commanders in their particular fields. One text deals specifically with incident command in prisons, albeit within an American context.[53]

49. B MURRAY (1994) Training for Operational Command, Fire Professional, Autumn p67-71.
50. Prison Disturbance April 1990. Report of an inquiry (Woolf Report) (1991) Cmmd 1456. HMSO: London.
51. FLIN (1996) op cit, p42-44.
52. Op cit, p229.
53. FREEMAN (1996) op cit.

Sui generis - **Prison management competence**

The fourth element of being a governor is that of having prison management competence. It is this element of a governor's work that is the most difficult to define. The incident command, general management and public sector management competencies have to be contextualised to reflect the penal setting. However, prison management competence is more than being able to undertake these tasks in a prison. It also involves more than the acquisition of prison specific technical knowledge and skills, such as how to conduct adjudications, undertake risk assessments and authorise release on temporary licence.

Most American literature on governing focuses on management styles, problem solving techniques and decision making approaches.[54] One author on American wardens concluded that 'I found strong, politically astute leadership, an organisational culture built around 'security first' goals and a paramilitary organisational structure more associated with higher levels of order, amenity and service behind bars'.[55]

Another concluded that wardens achieve 'quality incarceration' by 'imparting respect for the rights of others amongst staff and inmates; assure fair and reasonable application of the rules and regulations; value the lawful and reasonable relationships among people and provide the opportunity for personal growth in an environment without bias or hostility'.[56] It is this last quotation which comes closest to identifying the prison management competence required of prison governors.

One of the key facets of prison management competence is the ability to balance security, control and justice in prison. Lord Justice Woolf's inquiry into the causes of the 1990 prison disturbances found that

> 'There are three requirements which must be met if the prison system is to be stable. They are security, control and justice. There are two basic rules if these requirements are to be met. They are: sufficient attention has to be paid to each of the requirements; and they must be kept in balance. If this is not

54 . See for example M McSHANE and F WILLIAMS (1993) The Management of Correctional Institutions. Garland Publishing New York.

55. J DiIULIO (1991) Understanding Prisons. Law and Social Inquiry, Vol 16, pp65-99.

56. K WRIGHT (1994) Effective Prison Leadership, William Neil Publishing, New York, p123.

done, then the system is unstable and so is more prone to disturbance and riot. The April 1990 disturbances were a consequence of the failure of the prison system to conform with these basic rules'.[57]

We would argue that governors must be able to craft prison culture (both prison staff sub-culture and prisoner sub-culture); blend elements of legitimacy based control (humane regime, justice and fair treatment) with elements of situational control (management, design and manipulation of the prison environment); rapidly switch to a command role when appropriate; maintain a highly visible profile in the prison; demonstrate clear values and beliefs in order to demonstrate what is and is not acceptable behaviour; exercise power and decision making based on a firm moral foundation; effectively channel extreme emotions and feelings of prisoners and staff; and manage cultural, relational and discretionary elements of the prison environment.

The Review of the Prison Service which took place in 1997 identified similar elements, including: dealing with difficult prisoners; guarding against staff abusing their power; ensuring that staff exercise their authority legitimately and fairly; and maintaining a proper balance between the legitimate expectations of staff on the one hand and prisoners on the other.[58]

The environment in which governors have to operate is becoming increasingly more complex. The public outcry following the escapes from HMP Whitemoor and HMP Parkhurst has forced governors to focus increasingly on security and 'keeping in custody' those sent to prison. The reduction of more than 90 per cent in escapes from establishments in the past five years, despite the dramatic increase in the prison population, is a tribute to the professionalism of governors. This emphasis on security has had to be done at the same time as making efficiency savings.

These efficiency savings will continue to have to be made as £109 million needs to be saved between 1999 and 2002. The efficiency savings have led some governors to make cuts in staffing and regime provisions. However, governors have also had to manage growth and expansion in some areas due to an investment of an additional £226 million over three years for constructive regimes, including £76 million

57. Woolf Report, op cit, para 9.19-9.22.
58. Prison Service Review, op cit, p96-97.

for the Prison Service Drugs Strategy, an emphasis on improving basic skills and increases in offending behaviour programmes.

Whilst dealing with the security and regimes issues governors have had to launch major new initiates such as Home Detention Curfew which involves governors in detailed and comprehensive risk assessment, and the extension of in-cell television, which had implications for dynamic security.

Emphasis has also been increasing on working is partnership with other public organisations. Closer links with the probation service and other criminal justice agencies has resulted in governors becoming members of criminal justice consultative committees, Drug Action Teams and Youth Offending Teams to name but a few. Governors have also been encouraged to develop private sector links, to gain funding and support to workshops and other projects.

The governor therefore has to operate in an increasingly complex world, and has to demonstrate a wide variety of skills, if they are going to successfully manage risk, achieve security and change the lives of those in their custody.

CHAPTER 4

MANAGING PRISON STAFF

> 'The staff of the Prison Service are its most valuable assets. They are the means by which the great majority of services to prisoners are delivered. They are directly responsible for the custody and safekeeping of prisoners, for their fair treatment and care'.[1]

Governors form only a small number of the 43,000 or so people employed by the Prison Service. Within each prison are to be found uniformed officers, administrative staff and specialist staff including psychologists, instructors, nurses, doctors and chaplains. In addition to these directly employed staff are probation officers and teachers whose services are provided under contract with local probation committees and education colleges. Figure 8 shows the breakdown of directly employed staff by specialism.

Figure 8: Total Prison Service Staff: January 2000

Specialism	Number	Percentage of total Prison Service staff
Senior administrative grades	79	0.2
Governor grades	1080	2.6
Administrative grades	5602	13.0
Uniformed grades	29,814	68.5
Chaplains	217	0.5
Medical officers and nurses	1,246	2.9
Psychologists	476	1.0
Instructors, farm and technical staff	4,981	11.15
	Total	43,495

One of the key roles for the governor is to manage this myriad group of staff in order to adhere to the agreed contract for the prison. Manipulating staff sub-cultures, recognising the professional status of some groups whilst still managing their performance, ensuring equality of opportunity, crafting successful industrial relations and creating a

1. Home Office (1991) Custody, Care and Justice — The Way Ahead for the Prison Service in England and Wales. Cm 1647, HMSO, London, p35.

positive morale amongst staff are a few of the tasks each governor must undertake. This chapter explores some of these staffing issues and highlights the positive approach taken by some present day governors.

Staff culture

The term 'prison culture' is often used by researchers and commentators on the prison system when, in reality, they are referring to prisoner culture. As any sociologist would point out, a prison is made up of many sub-cultures of which prisoner culture is only one. The prison culture is therefore the sum of all the various sub-cultures within most prisons. Mapping and understanding the culture complex within a prison is a key part of a governor's role. They need to be able to recognise the existence of sub-cultures, understand the power balance between the cultures and to manipulate culture to achieve the prison's goals. This applies equally to staff culture as it does to prisoner culture.

The concept of culture, as it is viewed in organisational studies, derives from social anthropology, in which it refers to a community's shared way of life including shared values and symbols. Staff culture can therefore be described as the signs, symbols, myths, rituals and common patterns of behaviour ('the way we do things around here') found amongst a group of people. This group will have shared values, common beliefs and attitudes. Some of these will be observable and conscious and others not. From this definition it will be clear that there will be no homogeneity in prison staff culture. Different groups of staff have different cultures. Some staff sub-cultures are much stronger than other staff sub-cultures because of the level of turnover of staff, the closeness of the working relationship and the operating environment within the prison. The prison officer sub-culture is generally accepted as being particularly strong compared to, for example, the probation officer sub-culture. Where a strong cub-culture exists it tends to be learnt in an indirect manner through the work environment and can overcome any management 'cultural indoctrination' which takes place during initial training and induction There has been a growing body of research which suggests that cultures can be viewed as a 'controllable variable' and can be manipulated and managed to ensure improved organisational performance.[2] It is argued that effective sub-cultures are

2. A useful introductory text on the subject is R KILMANN, M SAXTON and R SERPA (1985) Gaining Control of the Corporate Culture, San Francisco: Jossy Bass. For an alternative view, which argues that the culture cannot be manipulated see L MEEK (1992) Organisational Culture: Origins and Weaknesses in G SALAMAN (ed) Human Resource Strategies, London: Sage).

likely to result when there is an alignment between, on the one hand, organisational values and strategic goals and, on the other, the values and work goals to which individual staff members are internally committed and which intrinsically motivate them. Any attempt by a governor to change an individual's values and belief system is unlikely to be successful. Culture change should therefore focus on changing behaviour. The issue of changing culture will be explored more fully in Chapter 10.

Equality of opportunity

Equality of opportunity is one of the Prison Service's Principles.[3] In seeking to achieve its Objectives the Prison Service has stated that it is committed to equality of opportunity and the elimination of discrimination on improper grounds. The Prison Service policy is within the broader Home Office policy of equal opportunities:

> 'The Home Office has a policy of equality of opportunity for all its staff, which has been agreed with the Home Office Trade Union side. The only factors which are relevant for employment and advancement are the individual's ability, qualification and suitability for the work or post in question. The Department is committed to the principle that all Home Office staff are given an equal opportunity for training, developing and advancement so that they can contribute to the Department's work to the full extent of their abilities and enjoy the full benefits of that contribution. The Department therefore takes decisions about its own staff and applicants for employment on the basis of evidence about performance and potential. It takes specific steps to promote equality of opportunity and to guard against discrimination (whether direct or indirect, conscious or unconscious) on grounds of ethnic origin, religious belief, sexual orientation, disability or any other relevant factor.'[4]

The Prison Service, like other employers, has a duty, created by the Sex Discrimination Acts 1975 and 1986, Race Relations Act 1976 and Disability Discrimination Act 1995, to prevent discrimination and

3. A copy of the Prison Service's Purpose, Aims, Objectives and Principles can be found at Appendix 1.
4. Home Office Notice 158/191 Equal Opportunities in the Home Office.

harassment. However, a 1994 staff survey, subsequent research and recent industrial and employment tribunal cases have all indicated that sexual and racial harassment and discrimination on improper grounds constitute a significant problem within the Service.

In an attempt to eradicate the problem the then Executive Committee of the Prisons Board and Prison Service Trade Unions worked together to produce a guidance document entitled 'Combating Harassment and Discrimination' which was launched in July 1996.[5] The guide contains comprehensive information and advice about the law on harassment and discrimination, definitions and examples of unacceptable conduct, responsibilities of staff and managers and the processes for making and dealing with complaints.

The role of the governor, as employer, is made quite clear by the legislation. It is unlawful for any employer to instruct employees to discriminate or to put pressure on employees to discriminate. In law the employer is responsible for the actions or omissions of all employees - whether or not they are known or approved - which occur in the course of employment and this responsibility can relate to situations outside the workplace if connected with a person's employment. Governors will therefore always be held responsible for any unlawful discrimination unless they can show that they have taken all reasonable steps to prevent it. The guidance notes make clear the important impact governors can have on the ethos within their establishment:

> 'Governors therefore have a crucial role in promoting a healthy and harmonious working environment for their staff which reflects the Service's commitment to equality of opportunity as one of its values. Managers should lead by example, by treating people fairly and equitably and thus demonstrating a personal commitment to equal opportunities policies. They should ensure that they are aware of any discrimination problems and should be responsible for ensuring that proper standards of conduct are achieved and maintained. They should be ready to investigate any apparent harassment or discrimination which comes to their attention, whether through a complaint or by other means.'

5. Prison Service Notice to Staff 23/1996.

The guidance document goes on to specify that governors, and indeed all managers should:

- encourage a working environment which welcomes diversity and is supportive of all staff;
- ensure that they and their staff are aware of the Service's commitment to equal opportunities and of the standards of behaviour expected of management and staff;
- ensure that potentially offensive material is not displayed or circulated in the workplace;
- take prompt action, before any complaint is made, to tackle unacceptable language or behaviour; and
- be alert to signs that all may not be well within their team.

Despite the existence of policy statements and guidance documents the Prison Service still has a less than impressive record in a number of areas, which was recognised in a recent equal opportunities progress report.[6]

Among the matters of concern expressed in the report were:

- continuing difficulty for ethnic minority staff in progressing up the career ladder;
- failure by managers in some instances to comply with the policy on part-time working;
- sexual and racial harassment.

The figures for females in the uniformed grades in January 2000 are shown in figure 9.

Figure 9 : Uniformed grades - percentage of females (January 2000)

Grade	Total	Number female	per cent female
Principal officer	1,240	87	7.0
Senior officer	3,797	322	8.5
Officer	18,937	3,127	16.5
Operational Support Grades	5,840	1,474	25.2

6. Equal opportunities in the Prison Service Progress Report, 1 April 1995-31 March 1996, Personnel Directorate, December 1996.

The Prison Service has made little use of the 'positive action' which is permitted under the relevant legislation, unlike 'positive discrimination' which is unlawful. Positive action is connected with training or encouragement to take advantage of opportunities for work in which women or people of a particular racial group are not represented or hardly represented. In order to ensure a more effective implementation of the Prison Service's equal opportunities policies, governors were required, in 1996, to identify an equal opportunities officer for their prison and to arrange for all managers to receive one day's training on managing equal opportunities. Further, all staff were to receive one day's training on combating sexual and racial harassment.[7] The emphasis given to equality of opportunity in any prison very much reflects the orientation, values and level of commitment of the governor.

The Prison Service has made clear that it is determined to create an environment in which prisoners and staff can be confident that they will not encounter racial discrimination in any form. A new racial equality action programme (called RESPOND - Racial Equality for Staff and Prisoners) was launched in February 1999. Although the programme is focused on racial equality, it is hoped that there will be wider benefits in securing equal opportunities for other under represented groups.

The programme involves the appointment of a Racial Equality Adviser, national support and help with recruitment campaigns and training on equal opportunities. The RESPOND programme consists of five main strategies:

- confronting racial harassment and discrimination;
- ensuring fairness in recruitment, appraisal, promotion and selection;
- developing and supporting ethnic minority staff;
- ensuring equal opportunities for ethnic minority prisoners; and
- recruiting ethnic minority staff

The existing position, however, indicates that much work will have to be done if the RESPOND programme is to be deemed a success. Figure 9a shows that ethnic minorities are very significantly under-represented, in the Prison Service, particularly in management grades.

7. Prison Service Instructions to Governors 51/1996, issued 15 August 1996.

Figure 9a. Ethnic Minority Staff in Prison Service (September 1999)

Grade	Percentage	Grade	Percentage
Prison officer	2.8	Administrative assistant	7.0
Senior officer	1.4	Administrative officer	6.8
Principal officer	0.9	Executive officer	6.2
Governor grades	0.5	Higher executive officer	3.2
		Senior executive officer	1.2

Only a quarter of establishments employ a proportion of ethnic minority staff which matches or exceeds the proportion in the county workforce. Asians are the most significantly under-represented group (1.1 per cent compared with 2.6 per cent of the economically active population), especially in the unified grades. The Prison Service has set itself very challenging targets for the recruitment of ethnic minority staff, as figure 9b shows.

Figure 9b. Ethnic Minority Recruitment Targets to 2009

		Milestones			
	Target per cent	Current representation	2002 per cent	2004 per cent	2009 per cent
Service	7	3.2	4.1	4.9	7
Operational	7	2.4	3.4	4.4	7
Non-Operational	7	4.3	4.9	5.5	7

Conduct and discipline

The disciplinary arrangements for Prison Service staff were reviewed following Sir Raymond Lygo's recommendation that there should be a single set of arrangements for all staff in the Service.[8] An extensive consultation exercise took place with trade unions, and the Advisory Conciliation and Arbitration Service (ACAS) was fully involved in the consultation process. The new disciplinary arrangements, which were consistent with employment law and ACAS guidance, were approved by the Home Secretary and took effect from 1

8. R LYGO (1991) Report on the Management of the Prison Service, HM Prison Service.

July 1993.[9] The new code of discipline covered all Prison Service grades. It made clear the responsibility for discipline of line managers and set down timetables for completing each stage of the process. It provided for a single disciplinary hearing in the majority of cases which would be conducted by the governor or head of division. The key features of the new arrangements are:

- employers and managers must act in a way which an objective observer would consider reasonable;
- all disciplinary matters must be handled as quickly as possible; at various stages in the process, specific timetables are included;
- wherever possible, informal guidance or counselling should be regarded as the most appropriate way of encouraging a member of staff to improve their conduct. Only if this is not appropriate should there be recourse to formal disciplinary action;
- the code introduces new disciplinary warnings and penalties. The most common response to proven misconduct will generally be a formal disciplinary warning (oral, written and final written). Other the code must be applied in a non-discriminatory fashion;
- all disciplinary matters must be handled with discretion and confidence;
- there is clear line management responsibility for disciplinary action;
- members of staff must be informed of a case against them and allowed to state their case and to challenge any evidence;
- a member of staff may be assisted by a colleague or trade union representative at all times;
- no member of staff will be dismissed for a first breach of discipline except in the case of gross misconduct;
- there is a right of appeal against any disciplinary decision or penalty.

All members of staff were given a personal copy of the new code which made clear the high standards expected of Prison Service staff:

9. Notice to Staff 65/1993 Conduct and Discipline in the Prison Service introduced two documents: the Code itself and a set of detailed Management Guidance Notes.

> 'All members of the Prison Service are expected to observe certain standards of conduct. Indeed a positive commitment on the part of members of the Prison Service to those standards of conduct and strict adherence to them are fundamental to the successful performance of the duties and responsibilities of the Service. Any failure to meet them undermines the work of the Service.
>
> The commitment to upholding standards of conduct in the Prison Service must, therefore, be underpinned by disciplinary procedures which provide a fair method of dealing with alleged misconduct. This document sets out the standards of conduct expected of staff and goes on to detail in the code of discipline below the procedure for taking disciplinary action when conduct falls below that standard. The primary objective is to ensure that standards are maintained and to encourage improvement in individual conduct.'

The governor is responsible for deciding whether to take formal disciplinary action and for conducting disciplinary hearings for all staff in their prison, unless he or she is the line manager of the person under investigation or the person being investigated is less than two substantive grades below that of the governor. In the latter case a governor from another establishment will be asked to conduct the hearing. The standard of proof required at the hearing is that required for all employment matters, with the notable exception of the police code of discipline, namely 'the balance of probabilities'. The Prison Service is currently revising its conduct and discipline arrangements and a new Prison Service Order will be issued in the Summer of 2000.

Industrial Relations

The Prison Service framework document, which established the Service as an agency, made clear that the Director General was responsible for ensuring good industrial relations in the Prison Service and reiterated that the Prison Service would continue to operate Whitley arrangements.[10] More recently, the 1996-99 corporate plan indicated that one of the main steps to be taken to strengthen staff effectiveness (strategic aim 9 of the Service) was to 'work with trade

10. HM Prison Service (April 1993) Framework Document, Section 5.9.

unions towards an improved industrial relations climate'.[11] The 1999 - 2002 corporate plan also indicates the determination of the Prison Service to move towards a more partner based relationship with the trade unions. All parties would be committed to the success of the organisation; the building of trust, and greater employee involvement and a recognition of legitimacy of the role of each party.

The Prison Service involves trade unions and staff associations in a number of ways including: 'provision of information' both by regular written communication and by oral briefings; 'consultations' where issues and proposals are raised and views sought which management then consider; 'negotiations' involving 'collective bargaining' on pay and conditions issues or otherwise confer with a view to reaching agreements and 'participation' where both sides work together on a project to generate ideas or proposals, to develop a shared commitment. Examples include the Health and Safety (Consultation with Employees) Regulations 1996 which require consultations where any measure at the workplace may substantially affect employees' health and safety.

The legal framework for Prison Service industrial relations is contained in a number of Acts of Parliament. The first of these is the Trade Union and Labour Relations (Consolidation) Act 1992 which deals with the definition of trade unions; the certification of independent trade unions; the disclosure of information in collective bargaining; non discrimination against officials; what is meant by 'lawful' industrial action; the role of ACAS and the various codes of practice. The second is the Trade Union Reform and Employment. Rights Act 1993, which addresses the question of facilities for trade union members. The third is the Employee Rights Act 1996, which clarifies various health and safety matters.

The industrial relations situation was radically changed by the Criminal Justice and Public Order Act (CJPO) 1994 and the impact it had on the POA. The situation immediately prior to the Act was described by a former Director General, Derek Lewis: [12]

> 'It's [POA's] stubborn defence of restrictive practices, coupled with its belligerent and often threatening demeanour, which resulted in deep public prejudice against prison officers ... The POA must have been the last bastion of 1960s trade unionism.'

11. HM Prison Service (May 1996) Corporate Plan 1996-99, p2.
12. D LEWIS (1997) Hidden Agendas: Politics, Law and Disorder, London: Hamish Hamilton, p130.

The industrial relations climate had changed little in the previous years. The May Committee in 1979, recorded: 'That something has gone wrong with relations between staff and local and central management is undesirable - evidence of distrust, alienation and suspicions occurred too frequently to be seriously in doubt'.[13] Woolf noted, some 12 years later, that 'the May Committee's expectations and recommendations did not result in any long term improvement in industrial relations. Indeed, industrial relations became worse.'[14] However, Woolf took the view that industrial action by prison officers should not be made unlawful and recorded that the Prison Service did not advance that intention.

By the autumn of 1993 the POA started to 'flex its muscles'. In October 1993, following a ballot, the POA gave notice of its intention to take both continuous and sporadic industrial action over a number of issues. The continuous actions commenced on 5 November 1993 in the form of a refusal to admit prisoners delivered to prisons by the police, the private sector escort service and private sector staff. On 18 November 1993 the Home Secretary obtained a temporary injunction preventing the POA inducing its members to breach their contracts of employment. In December 1993 a second injunction was obtained when officers at HMP Preston nevertheless locked prisoners out.

Mr Justice May, in the November 1993 case, decided that because under section 8 of the Prisons Act 1952 prison officers have 'powers, authority, protection and privileges of a constable' the POA did not enjoy immunities under trade union legislation and may not, therefore, with immunity induce prison officers to breach their contracts of employment. Further, because prison officers were in 'police service' as described in Section 280 of the Trade Union and Labour Relations (Consolidation) Act 1992, the POA could not be a trade union. The certification officer then indicated his intention to remove the certification of qualification.[15]

The ramifications of this judgement were enormous. Lewis records that 'Governors felt a great burden being lifted from them now that the POA spell had been broken. Working together, Prison Service management and Ministers had given governors back their authority'.

---

13. Inquiry into the United Kingdom Prison Services (May Report 1979), Cmnd 7673, London, HMSO, paragraph 10.22.
14. Prison Disturbances April 1990 (Woolf Report) 1991, Cmnd 1456. London: HMSO, paragraph 13.230.
15. Home Office v POA (1993) The Times, 19 November 1993.

In order to clarify the situation following the case (which being a claim for an interlocutory injunction did not fully resolve all the legal issues) the Government decided to made appropriate provision in the CJPO[16]. The Act, which received royal assent on 3 November 1994, put industrial relations on a sound legal footing by:

- applying to prison officers and other Prison Service staff who have the powers of a constable the same employment rights as other Crown servants. The bodies representing these staff were given the status and immunities of independent trade unions (S126);
- maintaining the position that it is unlawful to induce governors, prison officers and/or prisoner custody officers (roughly their counterparts in privately managed prisons) to withhold their services or commit a breach of discipline. For this purpose a breach of discipline means a contravention of Prison Rules or, in the case of governors and prison officers, the code of conduct and discipline in the Prison Service. If inducements occur and loss results the Secretary of State may take legal action against the person or persons so inducing those staff for damages (S127);
- enabling the Secretary of State, after consulting relevant representative organisations and others, to make regulations establishing new procedures to determine the pay and pay related conditions of governors and prison officers affected by the provisions of section 127 (S128)[17].

Governors are required to adhere to a number of agreements in their interactions with unions and staff associations at a local level. The key ones are the Industrial Relations (IR) policy statement, local Whitley Committees and the procedural agreement with the POA.[18]

The term 'Whitleyism' is the name given to the main and long established system of collective bargaining between management and unions in the Civil Service. It had its origins in a 1916 report on relations

16. For a detailed discussion of the legal aspects of S 126-128 of CPJO (1994) see M WASIK and R TAYLOR (1995) Blackstone's Guide to the Criminal Justice and Public order Act, London: Blackstone Press.

17. The impact of the CJPO (1994) on staff was explained to Prison Service staff in Notice to Staff 450/1994, which also outlined their employment rights created by the Act.

18. Prison Service Notices to Staff 63/1989, 51/1975 and 78/1993 respectively.

between employers and employees by the Rt Hon John Whitley, which recommended ways of improving IR in the United Kingdom following years of industrial unrest. The Civil Service set up a Whitley Council in 1919, followed by the Home Office which set up its own Whitley Council in 1921. The three general objectives of Whitley councils, as set down in their constitutions are:

- to secure the greatest measure of co-operation between the employers and the general body of staff, with a view to increased efficiency combined with the well being of staff;
- to provide machinery for dealing with grievances generally;
- to bring together the experience and different points of view of employers and staff regarding conditions of service.

Governors of the larger prisons were required, in 1973, to introduce local Whitley committees. This was later extended to all Prison Service establishments.[19] The instruction provided information and guidelines on the setting up and operating of local Whitley committees and included a model constitution. Representatives of all recognised Whitley trade unions are entitled to sit on the committee and it should consist of the governor and not more than 13 members, six appointed by the governor and seven by the trade union side.[20]

The industrial relations climate in the Service improved following the implementations of the CJPO Act 1994. The Executive Committee of the Prisons Board and the POA National Executive Committee issued a joint statement, in April 1996, following an IR workshop with ACAS. The workshop agreed some simple machinery to examine ways to improve the framework within which they did business. The work fell within four areas:

- the need to establish and work within a clear framework for industrial relations. That framework must include the values to which both sides are committed;
- the obligations for officials to conduct industrial relations effectively, and the scope for joint training; the industrial relations machinery required; and

19. Circular Instruction 51/1975.

20. The Prison Governors' Association which was established in 1987 is excluded from the Whitley Committee as it has not been recognised by the Home Office Trade Union Side or POA.

- the most effective communications required, especially in view of the ever changing climate of the Prison Service.[21]

The joint statement concluded by stating that the Prison Service and the POA 'want to build on that [excellent work already being done] as the basis for moving industrial relations forward in a more equitable, positive and constructive way'. However, the Employee Rights Act 1996 is increasingly being used by unions to challenge what are perceived as being unsafe working environments. Unions are using section 44 (1) (d) and (e) to question minimum staffing levels in prisons and to argue that staff should not work in wings where their health and safety is in danger. Section 44 (1) (d) and (e) state:

> 'An employee has the right not to be subjected to any detriment by any act, or any deliberate failure to act, by his employer done on the grounds that ...
>
> (d) in circumstances of danger which the employee reasonably believed to be serious and imminent and which he could not reasonably have been expected to avert, he left (or proposed to leave) or (while the danger persisted) refused to return to his place of work or any dangerous part of his place of work, or
> (e) circumstances of danger which the employee reasonably believed to be serious and imminent, he took (or proposed to take) appropriate steps to protect himself or other persons from the danger.'

The industrial relations procedural agreement with the POA makes clear that disagreements should be resolved wherever possible at establishment level.[22] The governor has a crucial role in ensuring effective IR yet receives little, if any, training in negotiating skills and broader IR issues. This may be why so many 'failures to agree' are referred to area manager level. Managing a complex IR environment requires as much ability and strength of character as managing difficult prisoners. Despite the CJPO a number of IR incidents have resulted in

21. Executive Committee / POA NEC Joint Level Industrial Relations Workshop with ACAS - 23/24 April 1996. Published 30 April 1996.
22. Notice to Staff 78/1993.

the Prison Service coming close to taking out injunctions against local POA officials and governor grades having to staff prisons.[23]

The Labour Party on coming to Government did not repeal the CJPO despite suggestions that it would do so. The Home Secretary, Jack Straw, has made his position clear and is on record as saying that industrial action can have no more place in the Prison Service than it can within a police service and that he will not change the provisions of the CJPO. Since this announcement action has been taken to prevent industrial action on a number of occasions. For example, the Home Secretary was granted an injunction on 10 November 1998 to prevent prison officers staging protest meetings over their 2.7 per cent pay offer.[24] However, in January 1999 eighty-eight local POA branches held unauthorised meetings to demonstrate at the imposition of a 2.7 per cent pay award. As a result, the Prison Service went to the High Court and secured an injunction which required the POA not to induce any of its local branches or individual members to hold these unauthorised meetings.[25] The review of the disputes and grievance arrangements and attempts to implement new pay determination arrangements, which are underway, may help to improve the IR position in the Prison Service.

Managing specialists

The Prison Service employs highly qualified professional staff to undertake specialist work. Specialist groups include medical and nursing staff, chaplains and psychologists, who have often received many years of professional vocational training prior to working for the Prison Service. They have their own professional bodies to whom they have to account and their own codes of ethics. For governors they can pose a particular challenge as professionals are frequently able to prevent, deflect, or slow down management changes because they enjoy a high degree of autonomy in their work, often buttressed by legal or regulatory protections.[26]

Professionals usually work where a non-hierarchical ethos prevails and where accountability is through standards generated within their

23. For example, on 1 March 1997 Wormwood Scrubs POA members met in the club rather than work in the prison resulting in governor grades having to operate the prison. The dispute concerned the opening of a new wing.

24. Guardian 17 November 1998, p4.

25. Prison Service News February 1999

26. See for example J SCHRIESHEIM, M GLINOW, S KERR (1977) 'Professionals in Bureaucracies: A Structural Alternative' in P NYSTROM and W STARBUCK (eds) Prescriptive Models at Organisations, Amsterdam.

professional peer group. Governors, officers and administrative staff on the other hand derive their authority and legitimacy from above and are accountable not to their peers but to hierarchical superiors. These alternative bases of power and forms of accountability have generated many of the stresses and strains inherent in the relationship between governors and some specialist professionals.[27]

For many years the governor did not have performance appraisal responsibility for some specialist grades such as medical officers and chaplains. The functional specialism (the then Health Care Directorate and Prison Service Chaplaincy) retained 'management' of the individual despite their work being done in a prison hundreds of miles away. This created many examples of individual abuse by the specialist concerned and a lack of effective management by the governor. It is only recently that medical officers have been brought under the direct responsibility of governors.

> 'Since 1 April 1994 senior doctors in the Health Care Service have been relieved of responsibility for writing the annual staff appraisal on the senior medical officer: this has become the responsibility of the governor. Although doctors remain answerable to the Prison Health Care Service for their professional conduct, they are accountable to the governor for their day-to-day work and he has no line of accountability to the Health Care Service.[28]

Genders and Player equate the medical officer's increased accountability to the governor as the 'erosion of their authority' and as another incursion of 'the new managerial elite'. Most governors would view it as being the equivalent of the improved management resulting from the introduction of general management in the National Health Service.[29]

Medical officers may create particular operational conundrums for governors. For example, medical officers must certify that a prisoner is fit for adjudication; cellular confinement; transfer; certain employment

27. These issues are explained more fully, albeit in a different context, in L METCALFE and S RICHARDS (1990) Improving Public Management. London: Sage.

28. E GENDERS and E PLAYER (1995) Grendon, A Study of a Therapeutic Prison, Oxford: Clarendon Press, p208.

29. R GRIFFITHS (1993) NHS Management Enquiry Report to the Secretary of State, DHSS, London: HMSO.

and, in the case of older prisoners, PE. Many adjudications have not been proceeded with on medical grounds and it is the governor who has to explain to staff why no action has been taken against a recalcitrant prisoner. Medical officers can also prescribe condoms to prisoners. Staff have understandable concerns since they may be used to swallow drugs in order to hide them. Prison psychologists can be used in forensic, clinical and occupational roles. In an article titled 'What do Psychologists do?' Cynthia McDougall, then head of Prison Service psychology outlined the psychology statement of purpose and its staff by applying sound psychological principles and high professional standards to:

- the delivery of agreed organisational objectives;
- the understanding of individuals at the organisations;
- the design of strategies for change; and
- the evaluation of effectiveness.[30]

Governors can use psychologists to undertake individual casework with prisoners, to design, run and evaluate offending behaviour programmes but also to help them more effectively to govern the prison. Psychologists are increasingly being used to help manage institutional change, analyse the behaviour of groups within prisons and produce management data on the functioning of regime activities. Psychologists are heading the research planning departments in some prisons.

Chaplains, like governors, are appointed by statute. Section 7(1) of the Prison Act 1952 states that 'every prison shall have ... a chaplain'. The Act goes on to state, in S7(4), that 'The chaplain and any assistant chaplain shall be a clergyman of the Church of England' and in S9(2) that the chaplain 'shall not officiate in the prison except under the authority of a licence from the Bishop'. The Act also allows the Secretary of State to 'require the appointment of a Minister' of another denomination where the number of prisoners who belong to a religious denomination other than the Church of England merits it. From a governor's perspective the chaplain is often seen as the religious co-ordinator for the prison. They are used to manage a range of representatives of other religions as well as prison visitors and other voluntary groups.

30. HM Prison Service (1992) Perspectives on Prisons - A collection of views on prison life and running prisons, London: HMSO, pp30-32

Prison education underwent a major change in 1993 following the passing of the Further and Higher Education Act, 1992. It was decided that, in future, education services would be bought directly from education suppliers selected by competitive tender rather than the local education authority. This in itself was in line with wider government policies outlined in the 'Competing for Quality' White Paper.[31] The result of the exercise has been to allow governors greater flexibility in the use of education and more responsive programmes. Employment of more part-time teachers has enabled the contractors to respond to the changing needs of the inmate population very quickly. Governors have been able to vary their contracts to increase or decrease the number of education hours depending on demand and budget availability. Some have argued, however, that contracting out the service of education to private companies has reduced the role of the education staff. The move to more part-time staff has meant that many teachers are no longer willing, or able, to adopt as full a role in the prison. Many of the duties previously performed by education staff were no longer provided for under the education contract. The contract for education services was, for many governors, the first major external contract to be directly managed. This required new skills of contract monitoring and evaluation, albeit often through the head of inmate activities.

In terms of their role within the criminal justice system the most closely linked professional group to prison staff are probation officers. Probation officers are responsible for managing 'community penalties' to ensure effective 'punishment in the community.'[32] Probation officers also prepare pre-sentence reports for the courts and supervise prisoners released on parole licence.[33] The probation staff who work in prisons do so under an agreement between the governor and the chief probation officer of the local probation area. This agreement had its genesis in Instruction to Governors 30/1993: 'National framework for the through

31. For a discussion of education in prisons following the contracting out of prison education see Prison Service Journal 1993, No 91, pp 25-36 and 28, and I BENSON's article in Prison Service Journal No 94, July 1994, pp41-43, written when he was Chief Education Officer.

32. The term 'punishment in the community' and 'community penalties' were introduced by the Criminal Justice Act 1991, as an alternative to the more traditional phrase 'alternative to imprisonment'. The switch was intended to emphasise the government's desire that non custodial measures should be seen as demanding penalties in their own right. See M CAVADINO and J DIGNAN (1997) The Penal System, chapter 8 Non Custodial Penalties: 'Towards decarcertation or the Punitive City' for a detailed discussion of the non-custodial role of probation staff.

33. For a review of the changing nature of the Probation Service see T BURNET (1997) The Probation Service: Responding to Change, Probation Studies Unit Report No 3. Centre for Criminological Research, University of Oxford.

care of offenders in custody to the completion of supervision in the community' which was a result of the White Paper 'Custody, Care and Justice.'[34] The White Paper emphasised the importance of close co-operation and was to be used by governors as the basis for determining and implementing more effective local arrangements for the delivery of throughcare work; to formulate a throughcare business and development plan and to agree the seconded probation officer complement. By 1 April 1994 this 'agreement' had been converted by Instruction to Governors 31/1993, into a 'new style contract between chief probation officers and governors.'[35] The managerialist nature of the contract with the inclusion of budget estimates, performance indicators, specific inputs required from the probation service and management responsibilities made explicit the nature of the service provision relationship between governor and Probation Service. Governors, often for the first time, were able to specify what work probation staff should do and to what quality they should do it.

Uniformed staff

Prison officers, senior officers and principal officers, together with the operational support grade (OSG), form by far the largest group of staff in any prison. Their union is the most militant and their sub-culture the strongest. If the prison is to function correctly the uniformed staff must be well managed, their morale maintained and their talents harnessed into productive activity, by the governor and their senior team. Yet the staff survey carried out in 1994 found that: 20 per cent of officers were dissatisfied or very dissatisfied with their job; 18 per cent disagreed or strongly disagreed with the statement 'I feel proud to work for the Prison Service'; 58 per cent stated that they had been worried about their physical safety and 55 per cent thought that they did not work for a well managed organisation.[36]

Prison officers have a very considerable influence on the daily lives of prisoners as Stern has pointed out:

> 'The prison staff are at the very centre of any discussions about change or improvement in the prison system. They see

34. Custody, Care and Justice: The Way Ahead for the Prison Service in England and Wales (1991), London: HMSO.

35. Instruction to Governors 31/1993 introduced the Throughcare Business and Three Year Development Plan between Chief Probation Officers and Governors Guidance Notes.

36. Staff Survey 1994, HM Prison Service Briefing No 74, 6 June 1994.

prisoners every day, talk to them, listen to their complaints and problems and help (them), or ignore them, as the case may be. They, and not prison administrators, determine the atmosphere of a prison, the level of day to day fairness and freedom from harassment that prevails. They decide whether well-intentioned reforms will be carried out or subverted.'[37]

Prison officers are critical to maintaining the security of an institution, as well as ensuring that the daily routine occurs and that effective offending behaviour programmes take place. Research in the USA has found that officers feel threatened by prisoners, unsupported by their managers, isolated from other officers and define their roles in a highly individualised manner which is essentially detached from overall institutional concerns.[38]

Little research has been done on the history and development of the variously called 'dubsman', 'turnkey', 'warder' or 'officer'; the notable exception being Thomas' 'The English prison officer since 1850, a study in conflict'.[39] More recently Woolf outlined his view of the role of the modern prison officer:

'Management must make clear to staff that in a modern prison service, the role of the prison officer must not be confined to the unlocking of cells. It should be a skilled professional role within a disciplined service. It should involve constructive care of the prisoners. It should involve preparing them to return to the community in ways which will make it less likely that they will re-offend.'[40]

The changing role of the officer, into more than a turnkey, has taken place over a number of years.[41] However, officers are an expensive

37. V STERN (1987) Bricks of Shame : Britain's Prisons, Harmonsdswoth, Penguin, p76.

38. E POOLE and R REGOLI (1981) Alienation in Prisons: An examination of the Work Relations of Prison Guards/Criminology 19 No 2.

39. JE THOMAS (1972) The English Prison Officer since 1850, A Study in Conflict, Routledge and Kegan Paul, London.

40. Prison Disturbances April 1990 (Woolf Report) (1991), Cmnd 1456, London: HMSO, paragraph 13.9.

41. For a more detailed examination on the work undertaken by officers see S BRYANS (1995) The Changing Role of the Prison Officer in England and Wales, in The Keepers Voice, Vol 16, No 2 pp17-20: Ministerial views of the role of the prison officer can be found in P LLOYD (1993) The Changing Role of the Prison Officer: A speech by Peter Lloyd, Minister of State with responsibility for prisons, 15 March 1993, HM Prison Service.

resource and governors need to ensure that their time is used as efficiently as possible. Governors should also bear in mind the recent comments by Cavadino and Dignan:

> 'Woolf had surprisingly little to say about the basic role and attitudes of prison staff, despite the critical importance of these to the nature of prison regimes. All too often in the past, attempts to liberalise the prison systems have been obstructed and frustrated by the actions and prejudices of basic grade officers fearful of losing their 'authority' and 'control.'[42]

This view should be compared to the findings of recent research in dispersal prisons which found that 'the commonplace view of prison officers as a body of people who, at every opportunity, set themselves against the liberal and progressive policy changes proposed by those responsible for managing the Service' was incorrect:

> 'Prison officers are often less reactionary, and prison governors and administrators less progressive, than that caricature supposes.'[43]

A useful categorisation of the work of prison officers was formulated by Lombardo.[44] He categorised a prison officer's work as involving human services, order maintenance, security, supervision, and rule enforcement. 'Human services' encompasses a range of issues, from counselling prisoners on problems, ensuring prisoners get food and clothes and identifying and dealing with self destructive behaviour by prisoners.

'Order maintenance' refers to a policing function in which staff are expected to describe this activity as keeping the inmates safe from manipulation, intimidation, and assault by preventing fights, gambling, homosexuality and other activity which is against the prison rules. Vagg has described this activity as 'keeping the inmates safe from manipulation, intimidation, and assault by others.[45] 'Security' involves

---

42. M CAVADINO and J DIGNAN (1997) The Penal System: An Introduction, London: Sage 2nd edn.
43. R SPARKS, A BOTTOMS and W HAY (1996) Prisons and the Problem of Order, Clarendon Press, Oxford, p137.
44. L LOMBARDO (1981) Guards Imprisoned: Correctional Officers at Work. New York, Elsevier.
45. J VAGG (1994) Prison Systems - A Comparative Study: OUP, p87.

officers preventing escapes by watching and counting prisoners and searching. 'Supervision' Lombardo describes as a matter of ensuring that prisoners are ready to do whatever they are supposed to do, or be wherever they are supposed to be at the appointed time. In addition, it involves ensuring that cleaning and food distribution takes place efficiently and effectively. Lastly 'rule enforcement' is described as encompassing both placing prisoners on report for breaking the rule and detecting illicit activities.

Attempts have been made by governors to enlarge the prison officer's job (extending it horizontally by adding tasks, and increasing the variety of work) and by enriching the prison officer's job (enhancing it vertically by adding higher level, more stimulating and challenging work). In addition, less skilled work which did not require the expertise of prison officers has been contracted out to civilian staff or to operational support grades. Prison officers are still required to do the basic routine custodial work. They continue to do the locking and unlocking, walking the landings and making sure that prisoners eat on time. The systematic approach to these tasks ensures security and control in prison establishments and will remain a key part of prison officers' work.

In addition to the physical security (walls, locks, bars, fences, cameras, and in some places, dogs) governors now believe that 'dynamic security' plays a vital role in maintaining order and preventing escapes. Dynamic security involves officers interacting with prisoners, occupying them in purposeful activity and helping prisoners to face up to their offending behaviour. The main emphasis of dynamic security is on active supervision in place of more passive surveillance. Direct supervision of prisoners, by prison officers mixing and talking with them, has occurred for many years in some prisons, but it is only recently that officers have become involved in therapeutic work. Prison officers are now encouraged by governors to help deliver professional treatment and development programmes. Through leading sessions with groups of prisoners, prison officers aim to help them: confront the excuses which they often construct for their behaviour; create understanding and sympathy for their victims; and learn how to avoid offending behaviour in the future.

This new work (in the past the preserve of social workers and psychologists) is demanding and challenging but rewarding work. Prison officers are now involved in the sex offender treament programme, anger management programme, bullying strategy prevention work, suicide prevention work and alcohol and drugs groups.

Prison officers are taking the lead in sentence planning for prisoners. Personal officer schemes have been introduced where a named officer is linked with a small group of prisoners to help them with institutional adjustment and throughcare. The officer helps the prisoner to identify what work he or she will do in prison, what offending behaviour needs to be addressed, and what developmental needs he or she may have.

Officers also run pre-release and development schemes which help prisoners prepare for their return to the community. These schemes focus on life skills, especially in relation to accommodation, employment, and family relationships. Such work requires a high level of skill and dedication given the reluctance of many prisoners to get involved in sentence planning.

A recent review of the literature on staff-prisoner relationships by Liebling and Price summarised the job of the prison officer as being to:

> 'Maintain security custody, in a context where people are held in confinement against their will; provide prisoners with care and with humanity; provide prisoners with opportunities to address their offending behaviour and assist with day to day management in the complex environment of the prison.'[46]

Whilst prison officers often describe themselves as having no authority to make decisions, in reality, as Vagg points out, 'they had and used various means to exercise control over the daily work and to reach some accommodation with inmates.'[47] Despite the hierarchy and regulations to be found in prison, prison officers exercise an enormous amount of discretion. Examples are, answering cell buzzers quickly or omitting small pieces of information from verbal and written reports to senior staff, thoroughness of searches, speed of unlocking prisoners for exercise or association and whether to place a prisoner on report for breaking a rule of the prison.

The existence and use of discretion was highlighted by Liebling and Price who found that 'there is consensus amongst prison staff that their work consists mainly of 'grey areas' with small areas of clarity, despite the existence of an increasing number of rules and regulations'.

---

46. A LIEBLING and D PRICE (1998) Staff - Prisoner Relationships, Prison Service Journal, November 1998, No 120, pp3-6.
47. J VAGG (1994) op cit, p93

They point out that the diversity of circumstances encountered in prison make the use of discretion both inevitable and necessary but that there are 'no explicit principles and guidelines to aid staff in the exercise of the (largely underestimated) discretion they hold.'[48] One of the key roles of the governor is to set the boundaries for staff and help them understand where the parameters are for the exercise at their discretion.

This chapter has discussed some of the key staff who work in prisons. Governors must mould and shape the contribution of these players if the prison is to work well. This is no simple task as this chapter has attempted to show. Dealing with unions, staff associations and professional pride requires a multitude of qualities including: patience, resilience, resolve and the ability to compromise. Managing staff is only part of the job of governing. The next three chapters consider prisoners and how the governor should manage them.

48. Op cit, p4.

CHAPTER 5

PRISONER DIVERSITY

> 'It is important to remember that prisoners are not a homogeneous group. The main common feature which they have is that they are in prison, either accused or convicted of having committed a criminal offence. In respect of everything else they are as heterogeneous a group of human beings as one might wish to encounter'.[1]

Governing a prison is often about maintaining an appropriate balance between competing demands. Not only does the prison have to be secure, but it also has to help prisoners change. This is clearly difficult, as to do both requires setting different priorities, and using different skills. Nonetheless the requirement to do both is enshrined at the heart of the Prison Service's philosophy, best exemplified by its statement of purpose (see Chapter 1). Thus, under this statement, keeping prisoners in custody - preventing escapes - has a similar importance to the duty to look after prisoners with humanity, and to help them rehabilitate. Some criminologists have taken issue with the imprecise nature of the words 'humanity' and 'law abiding', especially in comparison to the rather clearer issue of 'custody'. Joe Pilling, it will be recalled from Chapter 1, attempted to clarify 'what precisely we mean by 'humanity'.[2] For example, as far as 'respect' was concerned, this was related to each prisoner's basic human dignity and worth:

> 'This has all kinds of application to the relationship between staff and prisoners. Respect is the basis of our race relations policy, for standards of privacy and for the way we respond to prisoners' requests. interaction and the way mundane routines are carried out. Respecting prisoners means addressing them courteously, by the name they prefer; asking not ordering; listening to what they are saying; being sensitive to their feelings about being locked up. The way we treat prisoners'

1. A COYLE (1994) My Brother's Keeper: Relationships in Prison in J BURNSIDE and N BAKER (ed.) Relational Justice, Winchester: Waterside Press.
2. J PILLING (1992) Back to Basics: Relationships in the Prison Service, p5-11 in Perspectives on Prison: A Collection of Views on Prison Life and Running Prisons (1992), London HMSO.

families is equally important and is in a sense a measure of respect or prisoners themselves. Respect engenders mutual understanding, trust and good humour even in the most trying of circumstances. It is the key to healthy relationships. It is the key to good control.'[3]

Pilling went on to provide similar explanations for each of the other concepts of his vision of humanity, reflecting the importance he attached to this idea in the management of prisons. However it is noteworthy that he ended his analysis of respect with the belief that it also provided a means of maintaining control. Pilling was well aware that there was a tension between the custodial duties of staff and those concerned with treating prisoners as people. He described this tension as 'uncomfortable', and reflecting 'in-built conflicts'.[4] In short, the needs of custody and maintaining good order meant that staff were required to treat prisoners, and their visitors, 'in ways which no-one would choose if humanity was the sole guiding principle'. For example, families, including children and babies, had still to be searched for contraband, and sometimes it would be necessary to have visits under closed conditions. What was important was to determine 'a continuum along which prisoners are allowed greater or less freedom to exercise choice and personal responsibility'.

'It is not simply a question of security or humanity and rehabilitation, but how much security is appropriate for individual prisoners. This will always require governors and their staff to make difficult judgements - judgements which invariably deserve support ... we are inevitably in the business of balancing the different elements of our Statement of Purpose.'[5]

Types of Prisoner

At the heart of Pilling's philosophy was a recognition that each prisoner was different, and as a consequence, within reason, should be dealt with in a way which was consistent with that difference. Equally this is, in part, reflected in various ways by the Prison Service itself.

3. Ibid p7.
4. Ibid p10.
5. Ibid p10.

'Dear John' by Peter Cameron

'A La Carte' by Peter Cameron

'Now Then' by Peter Cameron

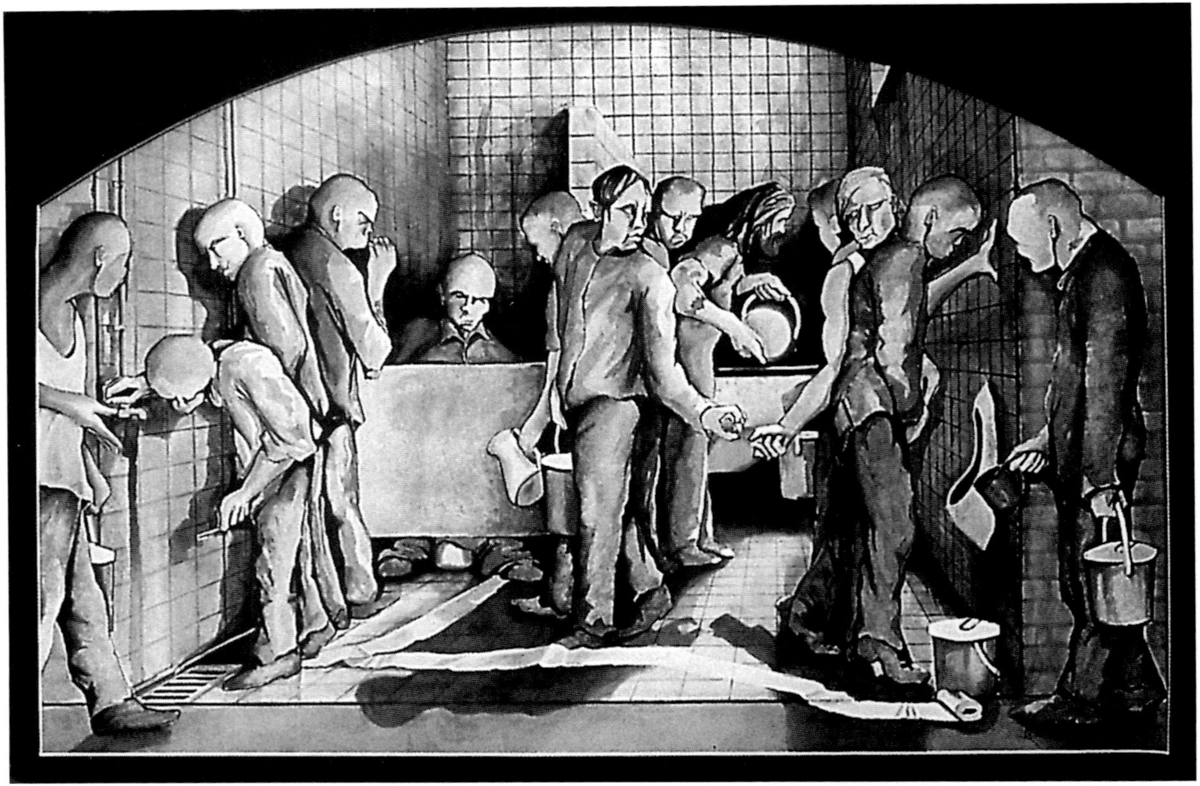

'The Last Slop Out' by Peter Cameron

After all there are different rules and regulations governing the treatment of, for example, young offenders, women prisoners, prisoners on remand, civil prisoners, and those who have been segregated for their own protection under Prison Rule 45. The need to maintain a balance within a prison's regime is underscored by the fact that one prison might hold several different categories of prisoner who are entitled to greater access to facilities, such as visits, or who, for example, are not required to work. Thus, at a very practical level, a prison which holds prisoners on remand, and those who are convicted, should have a visits room which is large enough, and systems in place to accommodate, prisoners who may receive visits every day, and all the consequent peaks and troughs at weekends when the majority of convicted prisoners receive visits. Similarly, a prison holding a large remand population would not generally provide work or education spaces for all, given that this category of prisoner does not have to work.

Perhaps the best way of demonstrating just how dynamic and diverse the prison population can be is through an analysis of the statistical breakdown of prison numbers from 1996. This is meant merely as a 'snapshot' of the dynamism of the number and type of people entering prison in any given year, and is merely illustrative given how rapidly things can change. Indeed, 1996's figures are already out of date given the dramatic and sustained increased use of imprisonment, as a consequence of Michael Howard's 'prison works' philosophy, and the subsequent passage of the Crime (Sentences) Act. For example, the average daily prison population in 1996, including all those on remand and convicted, young offenders and adults, women as well as men, was 55,281, a figure which was rapidly overtaken in 1997 and has continued to rise.

However, what is of interest for the purposes of this chapter is the diversity of those who make up this population. Thus, included in these figure were 6,722 young offenders, made up of 6,489 males and 233 females; 2,262 adult women; and 3,489 people serving life sentences, more than six per cent of the entire prison population. The lifer population includes 80 young offenders, and 124 women, of whom five were young offenders. This latter figure can be further sub-divided by offence, with the majority sentenced for murder but, for example, another 227 sentenced for sexual offences, including 191 sentenced for rape. Similarly there are different procedures for dealing with those who are given a 'mandatory', as opposed to a 'discretionary', life sentence. The numbers of those on Rule 43, now Rule 45, (own protection) were not kept for 1996, given the unreliability of the data, but it is believed that there would have been about 1,000 prisoners in this category. Nor are figures kept for those prisoners who are mentally disturbed, but a study conducted in 1991 found that some 38 per cent of the sentenced prison population, serving sentences of over six months, had some form of mental disturbance.[6]

Each of these different categories has specific needs which should be accommodated within a prison's regime. The difficulty of doing this is demonstrated by a NACRO report of 1993 concerning mentally disturbed prisoners held at HMP Birmingham. The report concluded that whilst a significant proportion of those being held had mental health problems, the reception process was inadequate for assessing mental disturbance; staff were inappropriately trained; and the health care centre, which was in any case not licensed under the 1983 Mental Health Act, could provide only the most basic care. In short, what the prison was attempting to do was to 'manage' rather than care for the mentally ill, and the prison was thus effectively isolated from 'general psychiatry, social services, and other 'helping' agencies'.[7] Similar problems arise when attempting to 'manage' the Rule 43 (now Rule 45) population.

Prisoners 'on the Rule'

The Prison Rules (1999), allow for the removal of prisoners from association. The first paragraph of Rule 45 is as follows:

> 'Where it appears desirable, for the maintenance of good order and discipline or in his own interests, that a prisoner should not associate with other prisoners, either generally or for particular purposes, the governor may arrange for the prisoner's removal from association accordingly.'[8]

6. J GUNN, T MADEN and M SWINTON (1991) Mentally Disordered Prisoners, London: Home Office. This figure has been disputed given that Gunn included in his findings those who were substance users / dependants.

7. Mentally Disturbed Prisoners at Winson Green: A Study of Staff and Prisoner Perceptions of the Problem at HMP Birmingham (1993), London: NACRO. All quotes taken from pp5-6.

8 There are various places to find copies of the Prison Rules. However, for a complete set, with commentary and comparison with comparable European Prison Rules, see N LOUCKS (ed) from the original by J PLOTNIKOFF; Prison Rules: A Working Guide (1993), London: PRT.

Thus it is clear that there are two reasons that governors might want to apply this Rule. First, they can use it to remove prisoners who are disrupting the prison's regime - for 'good order and discipline'; and, secondly, some prisoners need to be segregated for 'their own interests'. These two reasons are sometimes shortened to Rule 45 (GOAD) - good order and discipline - and Rule 45 (OP) - own protection. Typically this latter category will include those prisoners who are accused, or convicted of sexual offences. However, those requesting Rule 45 (OP) are many and various: from those prisoners who have found themselves in debt to other prisoners to those who have been accused of 'grassing' - providing information to prison staff about others.

The use of Rule 45 (GOAD) has had a chequered history, and has been described as the 'most controversial of the English Prison Rules'.[9] However issues related to the management of those prisoners on Rule 45(OP) are no less difficult, and are perhaps worthy of greater scrutiny given that they pose distinct problems in almost every prison. Indeed not only do they provide managerial difficulties for governors in almost every regime activity, from the provision of visits to access to the prison's chapel, but they are also a visual expression of a hierarchy devised largely by prisoners themselves, albeit often tacitly supported by prison staff. This hierarchy sees armed robbers - 'blaggers' - at the apex, with 'nonces' - sex offenders on the lowest rung. The poet Ken Smith gave a vivid description of this hierarchy, in the book of his experiences as writer-in-residence at HMP Wormwood Scrubs:

> 'A prisoner can be unpopular, a pest, a scrounger, a loony, a dog-end man, a whiner, a bully, a paranoid schizophrenic, a brown tongue, a back room [sic] lawyer, a thief or even a bit of a grass, but the worst he can be - here or anywhere - is a nonce. The fact is that a prisoner can also be a decent human being but, irrespective of character, a man's life in prison often depends on where he stands in the rigid hierarchy of prison values that descend downwards to the nonce. Everyone but the nonce gets to look down on someone else.'[10]

The management of what was, under the old Rules, the Rule 43 (OP) population was the subject of a major review in 1989, and whose

9. Ibid p100.
10. K SMITH (1989) Inside Time, London: Harrap, p46.

conclusions found expression in a government White Paper published in 1991.[11] The aim of the review was, in one sense, to destroy the hierarchy so graphically described by Smith. As a 'guiding principle' the Prison Service review of the management of vulnerable prisoners stated that governors and their staffs should ameliorate the worst effects of segregation under the Rule by ensuring that 'the regime for segregated prisoners should be as balanced and well integrated as for the rest of the population within the limits of affording them protection and maintaining good order and discipline, and nothing less than that.'[12]

This is of course another demand for 'balance' and some might argue that this is easier to say than do. How do you integrate Rule 45 (OP) prisoners, most of whom are popularly associated by other prisoners with sex offences, into a church service where, for example, the communion cup is to be shared? The review indicates that such prisoners 'must have the opportunity for corporate worship with others of their faith' and noted that this would mean 'special seating arrangements which, in practice, means either bringing the 45 population in first or last, having them supervised by a member of the discipline staff, and having them leave first, or after the other prisoners have left.'[13] This latter course of action often leads the non-Rule 45 (OP) population to complain that they are being disadvantaged as the 'nonces' are getting preferential treatment.

Similarly there have to be special arrangements for access to the education and PE departments, the library, and work. Thus, in relation to education, the report recommended 'open learning', whereby subjects would be presented in modular form with tutorial support, based in the prisoner's cell. A comparable approach was recommended in relation to work, and 'cell hobbies'. In relation to PE the report recognised that the small numbers involved, in comparison to the rest of the population, 'make it difficult to justify denial of the gym to a much greater number', given that 'prisoners are quick to spot this and their hostility can be a strong discouragement, to the provision of such facilities for Rule 45 (OP) prisoners'. The report therefore recommended

11. See The Management of Vulnerable Prisoners: Report of a Prison Department Working Group, May 1989; and Custody, Care and Justice: The Way Ahead for the Prison Service in England and Wales (1991), London: HMSO.

12. Ibid p48.

13. Ibid p4414. All quotes and references taken pp 42-45.

that there should be a published PE programme, and that PE could be offered on the Wing housing such prisoners.[14]

John May, in 1990 governor of HMP Dartmoor, recognised the inherent difficulties described above in managing the 'own protection' population, in a speech commissioned by the Suzy Lamplugh Trust. He maintained that the 'historical reality' was that 'there is very limited access to the facilities of the prison; not only therapy, for example, but also television and socialising', and that such prisoners were a 'nuisance'. However, what HMP Dartmoor had done was to transform the nuisance into 'an opportunity' by creating a 'Vulnerable Prisoner Unit' specifically aimed at treating sex offenders. In so doing it had trained its staff to co-lead therapeutic groups with sex offenders; involved the probation and social services with the work of the unit; and canvassed for other sex offenders to come to HMP Dartmoor from other prisons in the region. Thus, in simple numeric terms, sex offenders made up 25 per cent of the prison's population, and issues related to access to facilities became less difficult to justify. All of this brought different problems, with May believing that 'these people are very demanding of resources', and as a consequence his staff team had been 'overwhelmed'. Moreover opening the unit had done nothing to improve the attitudes of other prisoners, or staff, to sex offenders, but had merely 'polarised' opinion, and this is something to be addressed.[15]

Security categories

By far the most obvious way that difference is measured for prison staff relates to a prisoner's security category. The current categorisation system was introduced in 1966 (see Chapter 1) as a means of reducing the number of escapes from prison. Clearly prisoners in the lowest security category - category D - will be managed in ways which are quite different from those who are in category A. Category A is especially of interest as it is the only category that can apply to all prisoners, whether male, female, juvenile, sentenced, or on remand. The need for balance within the regime again becomes paramount if a prison holds different categories of prisoners. Does the governor manage all prisoners as if they are in the highest security which he or she holds, or are systems developed which recognise their difference? If

14. Ibid. All quotes and references taken from pp42-45.

15. See Working with the Sex Offender: Issues for Policy and Training, Prevention and Treatment, a Report of the Conference held on 29 March 1990 at Regent's College, London (1990), London, the Suzy Lamplugh Trust, pp9-10.

the latter strategy is chosen, what safeguards have to be established so as to ensure that security is maintained? After all it is very difficult visibly to distinguish between a prisoner who is, for example, a category B, and one who is a category D.

On the other hand it is not difficult to tell which prisoners are in category A, or those on the escape list. 'E men', as the latter are known, are required to wear a prison uniform with yellow patches on the jacket, and a yellow stripe on their trousers. They are also required to place all their clothes, with the exception of their nightwear, outside their cells at night. In relation to internal security procedures for category A prisoners, and it should be remembered that there are three categories of category A, all will be photographed, and their picture held in the security office and at the local police station. Similarly, they will be kept in the most secure single cell available, which in practice means not at the end of a landing, or on the top landing, and their cell location will be changed frequently. A continuous record of their cell locations, and their movement in and around the prison is also kept. Movement, even inside the prison, poses distinct difficulties as category A prisoners are always supervised by a member of staff, who is in radio contact with the communications room, and is sometimes accompanied by a dog patrol. Similar difficulties exist in relation to their access to education, PE, religious services, who is allowed to visit, and the conduct of visits.[16]

The implications for a prisoner being placed on category A are therefore far reaching, and will ultimately result in the prisoner being transferred to one the country's dispersal prisons, or HMP Belmarsh. One former category A prisoner - 'Alex' Alexandrovich - recalls some of the benefits and disadvantages of being an 'A' man:

> 'At ten o'clock I heard the night screw coming round switching the cell lights off. When he got to my cell however, he turned out the main light, but left the red night light on. Immediately I jumped up and knocked on the door. The night screw came back and I asked him to turn the red light off. He said that I was an 'A man' and the regulations said that the red light had to be left on. I was about to argue, but thought better of it.'

16. Issues related to the management of Category A prisoners are contained in HM Prison Service's Manual on Security. A good introduction to these issues can be found in S CREIGHTON and V KING (1995) Prisoners and the law, London: Butterworths p 439.

However, Alexandrovich was to discover some benefits of being an 'A man' after his transfer to HMP Wakefield, and vividly reconstructs the prison hierarchy described by Ken Smith:

> 'perversely, the fact that I had been put on the A list was in itself degree of protection because, in the prison hierarchy, a category A man was at the very top, respected the most.'[17]

Category A prisoners not only complain about their night light being left on, but also about visiting restrictions and maintaining family contact, given that they are moved on a regular basis.

Females, lifers and young offenders

Female prisoners, those sentenced to life imprisonment, and young offenders all have specific requirements which should be accommodated whilst in custody. All have been the subject of much research and discussion. What follows is therefore not intended as a major contribution to increasingly lively fields of enquiry, but is merely a reminder that the differing needs of these significant groups should be acknowledged, and accommodated by prison governors and staff. This is no small matter, as it is probably fair to conclude that until relatively recently female prisoners, for example, were managed as if they were 'cons in skirts'.

Female prisoners in particular have, especially in the past ten years, become widely studied, although this does not seem to have greatly affected how they are treated inside.[18] Issues related to the incarceration of women have again become more focused, given the rapid increase in the number of women, especially girls, currently being imprisoned. Of particular interest is a recent report by Sir David Ramsbotham, the Chief Inspector of Prisons, who concluded that the women's prison system should be managed as an entity through a single Prison Service Director, with responsibility and accountability for all that happens within it. This recommendation specifically recognises that the prison

17. A ALEXANDROVICH, and D WILSON (1999) The Longest Injustice: The Strange Story of Alex Alexandrovich, Winchester: Waterside Press, pps 28 and 46.

18. See, for example, P CARLEN (1990) Alternatives to Women's Imprisonment, Milton Keynes: Open University Press. P CARLEN and A WORRALL (1987) Gender, Crime and Justice, Milton Keynes: Open University Press; L GELSTHORPE (1989) Sexism and the Female Offenders, Hants: Gower; and NACRO (1996) Women Prisoners: Towards a New Millennium, London: NACRO.

regime requirements of women are different from those of men.[19] For example the report confirmed much of the criminological data that the majority of women in prison had never been in prison before; were mothers of children under the age of 16; had accommodation problems and a poor employment record; were serious drug misusers; and had harmed themselves or attempted suicide.[20] Thus 'women have different physical, psychological, dietary, social, vocational and health needs and they should be managed accordingly'.[21] This has implications for the selection and training of staff working with female prisoners; allocation procedures; and the type of regime that is required as a consequence. This can be practically difficult to achieve, especially in such prisons as Durham, Highpoint, Risley and Winchester which primarily hold men, but have units holding small numbers of women. To maintain a balance within the prison's regime in these circumstances demands much from all concerned.

A study conducted in 1990 found that there were more lifers in prison in England, Wales, and Scotland than the whole of the remainder of Western Europe.[22] This is of course a consequence of the sentencing policy for murder. The debate about 'mandatory' and 'discretionary' life sentences, and the tension between the executive and the judiciary in decision making about what constitutes 'life', has been well-documented,[23] but is beyond the scope of this book. What is of more concern is the impact that this large number of people has on the Prison Service, both in terms of the volume of prisoners in this category and in relation to their needs, given the length of their sentence.

Indeed this was acknowledged as long ago as 1989 by the Prison Service, in Circular Instruction 2/1989, which maintained that 'Lifers should be treated as a group whose special needs, because of the indeterminate sentence and the psychological and practical problems created by that, should be recognised'.[24]

There have been many twists and turns in relation to the management of lifers since 1989, but what happens to them remains a

19 Women in Prison: A Thematic Review by HM Chief Inspector of Prisons (1997), London: HMSO.

20. Ibid p16.

21. Ibid p26.

22. N McGEORGIE (1990) A Fair Deal for Lifers: A Study on Sentencing and Review Procedures for People Sentenced to Life Imprisonment in Western Europe, Brussels: Quaker Council for European Affairs, p23.

23. See, for example, N STONE (1977) A Companion Guide to Life Sentences, Ilkley, West Yorkshire; Owen Wells; and CREIGHTON and KING (1995), op cit pp 147-165.

24. Circular Instruction 2 of 1989, p4.

concern for the prison governor, and in particular the 'lifer liaison governor' in each establishment holding lifers. There are four main stages of a life sentence, which are intended to meet the changing needs of the system, and of lifers themselves. The first stage is perhaps the most demanding in relation to the resources of the prison. Following the imposition of the sentence it is usual for a lifer to be allocated to a lifer induction centre, such as D wing at HMP Wormwood Scrubs, or HMPs Gartree or Wakefield. However, category A lifers usually go directly to a dispersal prison. Female lifers go to H wing at HMP Durham, or HMP Bullwood Hall. Young offenders, sentenced to custody for life or detention during Her Majesty's Pleasure go to HMYOIs Aylesbury, Castington, or Swinfen Hall, but will be transferred to the adult system on reaching 21.

The purpose of this induction period is to get to know the prisoner, to allow a concentration of resources, such as psychological assessment, and to complete a risk assessment pro-forma. It is also at this stage that the prison receives the first written communication about the prisoner in the form of the 'confidential memorandum', and the initial life sentence plan, which will have been completed by the local prison where the lifer had been held awaiting sentence. These documents are used in the preparation of the life sentence plan, which takes account of the tariff or punishment element of the sentence, security category, training and medical needs, and domestic circumstances. In short it therefore summarises those areas of concern that the prisoner must address, or educational or work targets that must be achieved, in order to make progress through the next three stages, and on to eventual release. The life sentence plan also forms the basis of F75 reports on the lifer for more formal reviews by the Parole Board.

As is obvious from this brief summary of issues related to just the first of the four stages of a life sentence, lifers are worth their weight in paper.[25] Not only should this mean that staff are suitably trained in report writing and risk assessment, but it also requires time for staff and prisoners to meet to discuss progress and change. This is no simple matter, and for staff, keeping up with the relevant legislation and documentation can be difficult. In 1994, for example, five per cent of all Prison Service Instructions and Advice to Governors related to life

25. A very helpful book on the life sentence was produced by R Farrow, a probation officer working at HMP Blundeston. This simply explains the other three stages of the life sentence. See R FARROW (1992) The Life Sentence: A Guide to the Sentence for the Families and Friends of Life Sentenced Prisoners, Blundeston and Suffolk Probation Service.

sentenced prisoners, and their management. Moreover, given their uncertainty out release, the long term which will be served, and the knowledge of the gravity of the offence they have committed, all mean that life sentence prisoners experience much higher levels of stress than the prison population as a whole. Staff often comment that they like working with lifers, especially as many 'just want to get their heads down', and given the slow turnover of prisoners, relationships between staff and lifers tend to be more intense than in other prisons.

A different approach is required when dealing with young offenders. Indeed almost from the origin of the modern Prison Service young offenders have been seen as having special needs. It might be argued that those viewing these needs have oscillated between an agenda of punishment, in the form of the 'short, sharp, shock' and 'boot camps', to a more rehabilitative ethos, perhaps best symbolised by the borstal system. Ironically, much of the writing about the treatment of young offenders by Prison Service staff has also reflected this punishment/rehabilitation dichotomy, of late finding expression in individual establishments' attempts to combat bullying. HMYOI Lancaster Farms, and HMP Cardiff, for example, have produced excellent anti-bullying strategies,[26] both reflecting a 'whole prison' approach, which emphasises that 'the regime must be viewed as a positive response aimed at helping prisoners address their offending behaviour - both inside and outside the prison'.[27]

This emphasis on the regime for young offenders is enshrined in the rules governing Young Offender Institutions. Young offenders should have 'positive regimes' reflecting Rule 3 of the Young Offender Institution Rules of 1988 which states that 'the aim of a young offender institution shall be to help offenders to prepare for their return to the outside community'.[28] Brookes saw this Rule coming to life through the provision of work and education, designed to foster personal responsibility, and the chance to acquire skills which could be turned into a job; links between the offender and the community; and co-operation between the establishment and the probation service. The Prison Reform Trust believed that HMYOI Lancaster Farms in particular was an example of best practice in relation to the treatment of

26. Anti-Bullying Resource and Information Booklet, Leyhill: PES, and D TATTUM and G HERDMAN, Bullying: A Whole Prison Approach (1995), Cardiff: Cardiff Institute of Higher Education.

27. D P TATTUM and G HERDMAN (1995), op cit P 24.

28. P BROOKES ((1995) Positive Regimes for Young Offenders, in A Good and Useful Life: Constructive Prison Regimes (1995), London: The Prison Reform, Trust, pp12-19.

young offenders, and drew attention to the specific training that staff had received from the Trust for the Study of Adolescence. As a consequence, as the then governor, David Waplington, commented, 'we all have to know about young people because that's why we're here'.[29]

In essence this means ensuring that there are suitable work and education programmes to combat boredom. Boredom is seen as fostering anti-social behaviour, and thus young offenders have to be encouraged to work. These programmes have to be linked into the possibility of employment in the community, and thus there should be a network of local partnerships. At YOI Lancaster Farms, for example, a local company, Badger Press, provides work for the establishment's workshops for three months of the year. The YOI's education department, in particular, had the second highest number of National Vocational Qualifications in the whole of the Prison Service in 1995.[30]

Incentives and earned privileges

One way that these complex and seemingly never ending categories of prisoners might be managed is through a system of incentives and earned privileges. The national framework for incentives and earned privileges, which specifically mentions the differing needs of lifers, women, young offenders, prisoners on remand, civil prisoners, and those on Rule 45 (OP), was set out in 1995.[31] The national framework makes clear that the aim behind the scheme relates directly to HM Prison Service's statement of purpose, and in particular the fact that prisons should look after prisoners 'with humanity and help them lead law-abiding lives in custody and after release'. It also acknowledges that the scheme is based on prisoners' behaviour and willingness to co-operate.[32] In effect, rewards, in the form of 'key earnable privileges', relevant to the category of prisoner being dealt with, are given to those who conform.

The national framework had to be translated into local schemes by each prison. These schemes are organised on the basis of 'basic', 'standard', and 'enhanced' regimes related, for example, to the number of visits that are given in each month, time out of cell, or permission for prisoners to wear their own clothes. Thus these schemes relate to the

29. Quote taken from C SPARKS (1997), Lancaster Farms, Preventing the Next Victim, London: The Prison Reform Trust. Lancaster Farms is discussed more fully in Chapter 10.
30. Ibid
31. Instructions to Governors 74/1995, p1.
32. Ibid

desire of the Prison Service to provide regimes which are 'constructive', 'purposeful', and 'positive', although, as the aims of the national framework make clear, in doing all of this it is hoped to create 'a more disciplined, better controlled and safer environment'.[33] This seems to echo the duality of intention in the statement or purpose, and some prisoners would argue that the incentive scheme merely provides another source of control and punishment. Similarly, Chris Tchaikovsky of the special interest group Women in Prison, reflecting the views of female prisoners, outlined a set of regime changes which prisoners would value which were substantially different from those within the national scheme. For example she reported that female prisoners wanted such privileges as the freedom to choose a female doctor, and a free incoming telephone line for children and dependants.[34]

It might also be argued that there will always be prisoners who will either refuse, or be incapable of conforming to any scheme based on earned incentives. How, for example, is a mentally ill prisoner accommodated within a prison's scheme, or how does a prison cope with a persistently disruptive prisoner? Governors still need to be able to address these different groups which might exist locally, and no matter how helpful any national framework might be, must continue to ensure that there is a balance within the prison's regime in doing so. In all of this the prison governor is helped by understanding the nature of the prison culture, a subject discussed in the next chapter.

---

33. Ibid p5.

34. C TCHAIKOVSKY (1995) Women's Prisons; Houses of Pain, or Houses of Healing? In A Good and Useful Life: Constructive Prison Regimes, London: Prison Reform Trust (1995), pp20-26.

CHAPTER 6

PRISONER CULTURE

> 'Drummer Boy Seven said to Number Three
> You're the cutest jailbird I ever did see
> I sure would be delighted with your company
> Come and do the Jailhouse Rock with me.'
>
> *Jailhouse Rock - popular song*

There is a richness to prison life that often escapes casual observation. The words of Jailhouse Rock, for example, make a clear reference to situational prison homosexuality which few will have noticed. Prison is so often viewed as controlled, ordered and homogeneous that even with over 66,000 people currently incarcerated, those with little experience of prison can be taken aback by what happens inside. Christopher Morgan, for example, began an exchange of correspondence with the life-sentenced prisoner Tom Shannon. After one series of letters Morgan acknowledged that 'everything you say is new and a revelation to me'. As the correspondence grew Shannon wrote about prison earnings, hooch, hustling, ghostings, grasses, racism, sharks, and sex 'with male whores', leading Morgan to conclude 'what terrifying places gaols are ... you don't realise that what seems ordinary to you is absolutely extraordinary to an innocent like me'.[1]

Morgan might have been helped by being able to refer to the first British dictionary of prison slang which was published in 1996,[2] which has 32 different words for 'prison officer' in its 2,500 entries, or by attending the Perrie Lectures of that year which were entitled 'Prison and its Cultures'.[3] Peter Cameron, one of the lecturers, was a Koestler Award winner for his stunning series of paintings depicting life in local and dispersal prisons. Some examples of Cameron's work are reproduced at the end of this chapter. It should also be remembered that in a large local prison, in addition to those discreet classes of prisoner

1. T SHANNON, C MORGAN (1997) Invisible Crying Tree, London: Black Swan Books, p17 and p105.
2. A DEVLIN (1996) Prison Patter, Winchester: Waterside Press.
3. The Perrie Lectures were founded in 1987 and are named in honour of Bill Perrie, a former Governor of HMP Long Lartin. The lectures are held each year at PSC Newbold Revel, and the text of the lectures is reproduced in the Prison Service Journal.

described in Chapter 5, there would be those from a variety of ethnic minorities.

Despite all this there has been a reluctance to accept that a study of prisoner culture has any criminological validity, or has importance in understanding how to manage prisons. As Anne Worrall has commented, part of this reluctance stems from a contemporary unwillingness to acknowledge that prison can operate as a 'community in itself', and as a consequence the need to understand 'the nuances of social interaction that constitute the reality of daily prison life'. This is all the more important for prison governors for, as Worrall observes, any attempt to control prisons or prisoners can only succeed 'in the context of a recognition that prisons are unique forms of social organisation with cultures and subcultures'.[4]

This reluctance to see prison as a community 'in itself' is a relatively new phenomenon. As early as 1940 Donald Clemmer wrote about prison culture, the existence of a 'prison code', and a subculture based on the direct experience of prison. Clemmer described the gradual process of 'prisonisation' which moulded people into prisoners, and the norms of prison life.[5] The two best known studies of prisonisation are 'The Society of Captives' by Gresham Sykes, and 'Asylums' by Erving Goffman, who again stress the distinctiveness of prison life, with its all-encompassing character, resulting in what Sykes describes as 'the pains of imprisonment' - the deprivation of liberty, goods and services, heterosexual relationships, autonomy and personal security.[6] In all of this prison was seen as possessing an 'indigenous' culture, which was essentially shut off from what was happening to the world outside.

Criticisms of 'prisonisation' have largely concentrated on how prison and prisoners relate to broader social, economic and political trends and developments, which continue despite their incarceration. After all, prisoners had lives and personalities prior to being prisoners, and the vast majority would return to those lives on release. Similarly they have visits from family and friends and access to radio, TV, newspapers and telephones all bringing news of, and contact with, the outside world. As such, in 1962 Irwin and Cressey offered an

4. A WORRALL, Of Rats and Real Men? Prison as Community. Prison Service Journal, November 1996, No 108, pp27-31.

5. D CLEMMER (1940) The Prison Community, New York, Holt, Rinehart and Winston.

6. GM SYKES (1958) The Society of Captives, Princetown: Princetown University Press; E GOFFMAN (1961) Asylums : Harmondsworth, Penguin.

'importationism' hypothesis, which maintains that the behaviour of prisoners is not characterised by their experience of prison at all, but by other cultures and subcultures which exist outside the prison walls.[7]

At the heart of these alternative models is the nature of power, order and authority in prison. In short, who is in control, and how is control managed? In particular three basic questions can be asked. Are prisoners' responses individualistic, or characterised by group solidarity? Do prisoners respond to the demands of prison, or as a consequence of their lives and personality from outside? Are their responses weak, and reactive, or can they have power to challenge and shape their environment in the face of what appears total control? These are important questions for prison governors who have to understand and often manipulate the complexity of prison sub-cultures.

Race and culture

The issue of race has played an important role in developing the argument and counter-argument in relation to prisoner culture. In particular Elaine Genders and Elaine Player were the first to demonstrate that race and racism had a major impact on the social organisation of prisons in this country.[8] In their analysis of attitudes towards race in three different (and fictitiously-named) prisons they were able to demonstrate that the previous mutually exclusive positions of indigenous and importationist theories could both have an impact on prison life, and should instead be viewed as complementary. The culture of the prison was dependent upon different types of structural conditions prevalent within that prison. Thus, for example, more rigid or authoritarian regimes tended to generate greater inmate solidarity, whilst less harsh regimes, which afforded prisoners some degree of authority, tended to diminish prisoner solidarity.

In attempting to understand how these theories would work in practice, Genders and Player considered the respective features of each prison, its role, and how it was organised. Thus, Littlebourne, the long-term dispersal prison in their study (in reality HMP Long Lartin) had a highly structured inmate society with a hierarchy of white, professional criminals at the top, most of whom knew each other prior to coming into prison, and sex offenders - or nonces - at the bottom. In this

7. J IRWIN and D CRESSEY (1962) Thieves, Convicts and the Inmate Culture, Social Problems, Vol 10.

8. E GENDERS and E PLAYER (1989) Race Relations in Prison, Oxford: Clarendon Press.

hierarchy black prisoners tended to operate as 'small businessmen' on the margins of the illicit prison economy. Thus the culture of HMP Long Lartin had elements of both indigenous and importationist cultures, reflecting prisoner solidarity as an outgrowth of long-term imprisonment, but roles within that culture were dominated by experiences gained on the outside. When the prison authorities attempted to interfere with this culture as when, for example, a tool went missing and the prison was 'locked down', old divisions would disappear temporarily and the prisoners would unite against the staff group.

At Newfield, by contrast, the young offender institution in their study (in reality HMYOI Huntercombe) a different story emerged. Once again the nature of the establishment itself shaped the pattern of inmate relations, based on the age of the young offenders, their relatively short sentences, and by the fact that the majority came from London. There was little organised illicit economy, reflecting the young offenders' lack of maturity; no particular hierarchy; 'power groups' tended to be fluid given the rapid turnover in population, and the fact that most of the young offenders - black and white - knew each other in the community. Thus elements of both indigenous and importationist cultures were again evident, although it might be argued that the institution's character was significantly more importationist given the relatively quick turnover of the population.

Most studies of prison cultures have concentrated on male prisons, and thus there is comparatively little written about culture inside women's prisons, although various contemporary studies have focused on the ways in which prisonisation tends to feminise, medicalise, and infantilise women prisoners.[9] Similarly there is comparatively little written about the impact that prison staff have on the culture of prisons. Indeed this absence is even more marked in relation to female prison staff. Whilst there is an extensive literature of 'cop culture' comparatively little exists in relation to prisons, which has meant that prison staff are more likely to be stereotyped and caricatured. This is unfortunate, for it is at best unhelpful, and at worst a serious misunderstanding of how prisons work and are managed.

The importance of culture can best be demonstrated by using examples of how normal prison routines and practices can vary from

9. See in particular P CARLEN (1983) Women's Imprisonment, London: Routledge and Kegan Paul.

prison to prison, and how different prisons handle similar issues but in relation to their own particular culture. Whilst these examples are anecdotal and not scientifically evaluated in relation to a recognised piece of research, they have all occurred within our working lives as prison governors, and thus can be used as illustrative of the importance of an understanding of prison culture. As such we have chosen examples which relate to a governor's daily routine, or issues which are generic to all prisons. The importance of a governor's routine was underlined by Trevor Gadd, who as governor of HMP Wakefield, commented upon the 'paramount importance' of the governor undertaking the daily round through the prison, maintaining a direct contact with staff and prisoners, and thus becoming 'the ultimate authority and source of understanding of the prison community'.[10]

Prison food

Food is a very emotive subject in prison. In local prisons and remand centres with their rapidly changing populations, and largely importationist culture, the prison's food is often judged against 'fast food' available in the community's fish and chip shop, McDonalds, or the Indian or Chinese take-aways. In long-term prisons or dispersals food is again a central feature of the prisoner's day, and the quality of the food a regular feature of prisoners' requests and complaints. Reflecting a largely indigenous culture, many prisoners react by becoming vegetarians or vegans in the hope of obtaining a better diet, whilst others put on weight through an unending intake of carbohydrate, or supplement their diet by buying tinned food at the prison's canteen. In some long-term prisons, prisoners are allowed to cook for themselves, and this led to much comment and debate as a result of food 'shopping trips' by staff on behalf of prisoners at HMP Whitemoor's Special Secure Unit.[11]

Tom Shannon's letters are filled with stories and fantasies about food. He dreams of coconut ice, regularly reads cookbooks and supplements his diet with tins of peaches bought at the canteen. He is also scathing about HMP Maidstone's kitchens: 'If you saw the food arriving here as a producer you would stand proud. If you saw it on the

10. T GADD, A little touch of Harry in the Night in J REYNOLDS and U SMARTT (1996), Prison Policy and Practice, Prison Service Journal, pp194-199.

11. Report of the Inquiry into the escape of six prisoners from the Special Secure Unit at Whitemoor Prison in Cambridgeshire, on Friday 9th September 1994 (Woodcock Report) (1994), Cmnd 2741. London: HMSO, pp64-66.

hot plate, you would weep. Something very mysterious happens to the food'.[12]

He is no less insulting about the food at HMP Albany, commenting, 'I don't know what it is about prison food. You eat it, and about an hour later you almost achieve lift-off, every 20 minutes or so'.[13] Prison catering managers might retort that, despite tabloid stories of excess and luxury, they have to provide each prisoner with three meals per day for less than an average of £1.40 per inmate per day. This is less than is budgeted to feed the prison's dogs.

Audrey Peckham is equally critical about the food in such prisons as Styal and Pucklechurch, and described, for example, an outbreak of food poisoning at the latter after eating chicken curry at lunch. 'I had better leave it to the imagination' she wrote, 'as to what it is like to be locked up with food poisoning, a plastic pot and no washing facilities'.[14] Peckham was particularly insightful about the centrality of prison food within a regime:

> 'It was surprising how important a place food held in our lives. Meal times broke up the day, marked the passage of time, and were a kind of focal point, something to look forward to. It sounds pathetic, but that's how it was: visits, letters and meals were all we had to look forward to ... The pre-occupation of prisoners with their food is a well-observed symptom, and although I certainly experienced it as much as anybody else, I still don't understand how meal times came to be of such importance. No doubt it was really all psychological - substitution or something of the kind. Yet as soon as one meal was over we would be wondering about the next.'[15]

Peckham worked in HMP Styal's kitchens, and most prisons' kitchens are a major provider of employment for prisoners. However, some of the original 'contracted out' kitchens did not initially employ prisoners, preferring to maintain their own civilian staff. This was the case at HMP Woodhill in 1991 when ARAMARK won the contract. However, this soon changed, and despite the potential security risks involved, a small number of prisoners were chosen to work with

12. T SHANNON, C MORGAN (1996) op cit, p21.
13. Ibid, p181.
14. A PECKHAM (1985) a Women In Custody, London: Fontura p58.
15. Ibid, p79.

ARAMARK's civilian staff, and continue to do so. Not only did this reduce the cost of the contract, but it also provided some crucial prisoner support within the inmate population for the food which the kitchen contractor was producing. In essence the prison kitchen workers would return to their wings, and counteract any rumours as to how the food was prepared, when it was cooked, and would return to the kitchen with comments and suggestions. This was no small matter given that the prison had been duped into believing that Muslim prisoners were being provided with halal meat, when in fact they were not.[16] Similarly ARAMARK's civilian staff could meet prisoners in a non-threatening environment, which in turn gave them greater confidence when serving prisoners on the wings.

Given all this background it should be remembered that as part of the daily routine, the governor or the duty governor is required to taste a meal. This is normally done in the prison kitchen, out of sight of prisoners, often at the optimum moment when the food has just been prepared, and despite the fact that the same food will not be served to prisoners for up to another hour. Further unreality exists in that it is common for 'the governor's plate' to be best china, and for 'real', as opposed to plastic, knives and forks to be used. The governor thus tastes the meal - and often it is no more than a cursory taste - signs the menu book, and continues on his rounds, deflecting any criticism of the food on the basis that 'I've eaten it myself'.

This is a far from stereotypical picture, and does little to enhance the image or reality of the prison's food, or manage an issue which is of great importance to prisoners. However, some prison governors deal with this issue in more positive ways, conscious of the culture of their prison, and how they might influence it. At some prisons, for example, the governor regularly tastes the meal at the wing hot plate, lining up with the prisoners to pick up a food tray and cutlery prior to sitting down and eating the meal with the prisoners at their table.

A similar approach was attempted at HMP Woodhill, but met with little success, as the basic prison culture was different from long term prisons, and merely resulted in scores of prisoners forming an orderly queue behind the governor grade concerned so that they could voice their complaints about the food. However, acknowledgement of the

16. One of the authors was chair of HMP Woodhill's Race Relations Management Team at this time. The issue of the non-provision of halal meat was taken very seriously, and resulted in the sacking of the kitchen manager of ARAMARK.

culture of HMP Woodhill's prison population, with its rapid turnover of prisoners, was eventually incorporated into the food by presenting the meals so that they looked like 'fast food', and increasing the amount of curries, and fish and chips. This may not have been ideal, but it did go some way in deflecting criticism of the food, and at improving communication between staff, inmates and the kitchen contractors. Subsequently a food committee was set up, and issues which had previously been a source of tension were discussed in an open and positive manner.

Visiting times

Another defining routine in any prison is the management of visits. As far as prisoners are concerned, Audrey Peckham admirably sums up the mixed emotions of having loved ones visit inside: 'visits were events to be longed for and dreaded. I was not the only one to find them intensely upsetting'.[17] Andrew Coyle, perhaps one of the most liberal governors of the modern era, understood something of the upset experienced by prisoners in describing visits at HMP Peterhead, in Scotland:

> 'Coming from Glasgow to visit 'her man' a woman, perhaps with one or two small children in tow, would leave home at the crack of dawn to make a two hour train journey to Aberdeen. She would then catch a bus which would take a further hour to get to Peterhead. The visiting facilities in the prison were primitive ... the visit, which would last for about two hours, took place in a bare room, more often than not with the partners separated from each other by a glass screen.'[18]

Coyle was to become Governor of HMP Brixton in 1991, and so was also able to put his Scottish experiences into an English context. His conclusion was that no matter how visiting rooms improved, with the provision of children's crèches and so forth, the only way in which to allow families to stay together was to 'allow prisoners to go home regularly for short periods of time'.[19]

17. A PECKHAM (1985) op cit, p102.

18. A COYLE (1994) The Prison we Deserve, London: Harper Collins, p95. A description of Coyle's work at HMP Brixton can be found in Chapter 10 of this book.

19. A COYLE (1994) op cit, p173.

For staff, visits pose distinct problems. Quite apart from the simple logistics of ensuring that the right prisoner gets called from his or her cell, and moved to the visits room suitably dressed and searched, there are obvious security risks involved when attempting to control large numbers of visitors and prisoners. Drugs are passed, alcohol consumed, and most worrying of all 'walk outs' - whereby a prisoner escapes pretending to be a visitor and leaves with them - take place. How can prison staff remain security conscious whilst at the same time attempt to ensure that the atmosphere within the visits room is as normal as possible?

There are of course other practical issues related to visits, and their management can often reveal much about the particular culture of the prison. For example, do Rule 45 (OP) prisoners have visits at the same time as the general prison population? Is property allowed to be handed out or in? Does the prison stick rigidly to the time allocated for remand prisoners? How is the search of visitors organised? Is there a Visitors' Centre, or a WRVS canteen? Is there a system of 'booked visits', and how are visiting orders (VOs) issued? Do staff walk amongst the visits tables during their period of duty, or do they tend to congregate together, almost oblivious to what is happening? Are visitors allowed to hold hands, or touch or kiss? Are the children of visitors entertained and looked after, or do they simply run around squealing, shouting and crying?

Various technological developments have significantly improved the security of the visits area. Closed circuit television (CCTV), for example, has markedly increased the degree of surveillance possible within the visits room. Similarly hand, finger and eye identification systems have been installed into most visits reception areas, which have cut down on the number of escapes through 'walk outs'. It is also interesting to note that visitors who were caught attempting to smuggle drugs into prisons tended to be visiting the prison for the first time. In other words, the visitor had little idea of the security which was available to stop them trafficking, and were as a consequence often extremely naive about what would happen. Similarly it was rare to find contraband on a visitor who had been visiting a prison regularly, suggesting something of how the prison grapevine worked and perhaps indicating which type of prison will have greatest success in finding contraband.

These issues are generic to all prisons, whether locals or training, young offender institutions, or those housing women. However they have a particular importance within the dispersal estate, and are especially acute within Special Secure Units (SSUs). An example of how these issues worked in practice was provided by the Woodcock Enquiry Team, who as part of their investigation into the escape from HMP Whitemoor's SSU, described the unit's visiting arrangements and procedures in less than flattering terms. After all, as the enquiry team concluded, 'the most logical, and most available, way to get items into a prison was to have a visitor smuggle them in'.[20]

> 'During visits, officers should have monitored visually and audibly. Originally it was envisaged that one officer would be in the visits room but this was changed to being immediately outside the rooms. In fact they normally sat together at the end of the main area, rather than looking into the visits room or maintaining mobility.'[21]

In short, over a period of time, staff had been conditioned into the culture of the SSU, and as such had accepted practices over time, in relation to visits, which in other circumstances they would not have allowed. They had moved out of the visits room, allowing the prisoner and his visitor complete freedom, and by September 1994 were no longer in sight or hearing of what was taking place. This was an extraordinary state of affairs, and may have accounted for the contraband which was eventually found in the unit and for the gun and ammunition which was smuggled in to effect the escape. All of this can best be understood by analysing the culture which existed within the SSU, and in remembering that prisoners also became aware of cultures. For, as has been alluded to, a study of penal cultures relates quite directly to the exercise of power - of who is in control. As one of the SSU staff put it, whilst inducting a new colleague about not entering the visits hall, 'sit down, and (do) not move about, as the prisoners don't like it'.[22] It is clear who was in control in HMP Whitemoor's SSU.

SSUs, by whatever name, serve a very specific function, housing in the main terrorist prisoners. Very few prisons require their level of security, and it is to be regretted that the general tightening of security that followed in the wake of the Woodcock Enquiry has affected almost

20. Woodcock Report, op cit, p35.
21. Ibid, p42.
22. Ibid, p42

every prison. However the events at HMP Whitemoor in 1994 do suggest the general importance of governors being able to understand, to shape and respond to the prison's culture if security and order are to be maintained.

What we have written with regard to prison culture is clearly not simply related to SSUs, and is merely a scant description of the richness of the reality of prison life - a reality which every member of staff who works in a prison would be able to describe.

CHAPTER 7

ENSURING JUSTICE

> 'A recurring theme in the evidence from prisoners who may have instigated, and who were involved in, the riots was that their actions were a response to the manner in which they were treated by the prison system. If what they say is true, the failure of the Prison Service to fulfil its responsibilities to act with justice created in April 1990 serious difficulties in maintaining security and control in prisons.'[1]

Woolf asked the prisoners who had rioted exactly what it was that they felt was unjust about their treatment inside. A content analysis of their comments, covering each establishment which had rioted in 1990, indicated five main causes of the riots; 'bang up', as opposed to association; the attitudes of staff; and complaints about food. The fifth cause which prisoners identified related to 'copy cat' behaviour, as news and publicity of the trouble at HMP Manchester spread. Woolf concluded that the concept of justice should be central to the work of the Prison Service. When justice is absent, problems emerge.

The issue of staff attitudes, as was explained in Chapter 5, should remind us that staff who work there have the power to make the lives of prisoners miserable. This is particularly true of governors, who can through the adjudication process, for example, increase the amount of time that prisoners spend inside; remove prisoners from normal association, and have them placed in the segregation unit and restrict their access to a range of facilities or privileges. These are significant powers, which have to be exercised with fairness and consistency, ensuring that justice is not only done but also seen to be done. As a former Director General of the Prison Service commented, 'justice as a concept, goes beyond having fair disciplinary procedures and proper channels for redress of grievances. It goes to the heart of the prisoner's experience of how he or she is treated.'[2]

1. Prison Disturbances April 1990 (Woolf Report) (1991), Cmnd 1456, London: HMSO, p226.
2. J PILLING (1992) Back to Basics: Relationships in the Prison Service, in Perspectives on Prison: A Collection of Views on Prison Life and Running Prisons, London: HMSO, p46.

In response to the findings of his inquiry, Woolf made 12 key recommendations and 204 proposals in the hope of preventing future trouble in prisons. Briefly they were:

- closer co-operation between the different parts of the criminal justice system;
- more visible leadership of the Prison Service by the Director General;
- increased delegation of responsibility to establishment governors;
- an enhanced role for prison officers;
- a prisoner 'compact' setting out the prisoner's responsibilities and expectations in the prison in which he or she is being held;
- a national system of accredited prison standards;
- a new Prison Rule that no prison should hold more prisoners than is provided for in its certified normal level of accommodation;
- a public commitment by ministers for prisoners to have access to sanitation;
- better community and family links for prisoners, through more visits and home leaves, and by being kept as near to their homes as possible;
- the division of establishments into smaller, and more manageable units;
- a separate statement of purpose for remand prisoners; and
- improved standards of justice inside.[3]

This last recommendation is worth quoting in full. It states that to improve the standard of justice in prisons would involve giving 'reasons to a prisoner for any decision which materially and adversely affect him; a grievance procedure and disciplinary proceedings which ensure that the governor deals with most matters under his present powers; relieving boards of visitors of their adjudicatory role; and providing for final access to an independent complaints adjudicator.'[4] The work of the Prisons Ombudsman - the independent complaints adjudicator - is discussed elsewhere (see Chapter 8), but the remainder of this chapter will deal with some of the consequences of this

3. Ibid pp433 - 434.
4. Ibid, p434.

recommendation, and its philosophical relationship to the 'justice model' when applied to the penal system.

Adjudications

Mark Leech, a former prisoner, writes in his autobiography of one of his appearances before a board of visitors adjudication at HMP Wormwood Scrubs in 1977, where he was charged with making a 'false and malicious allegation' against an officer, whom he nicknames 'Mudguard'. On the completion of the preliminaries to the adjudication, the security officer, who was acting as the reporting officer, slipped a note from the governor to the chairman of the board. Leech objected, and as a consequence the chairman read the contents of the letter, which described Leech as 'subversive, devious and disruptive who has made these type of false and malicious allegations in the past'. Leech again objected that this was inappropriate, which was duly noted; he was then denied permission to call defence witnesses, on the grounds that it would disrupt the prison workshops and was allowed only a few questions in his cross examination of the officer concerned. He concludes 'I was, of course, found guilty and sentenced to a further 35 days imprisonment by way of lost remission'.[5]

Leech, who read law to degree level and now works for a law firm in Liverpool, challenged this decision in the High Court. He won the case, earning himself immediate release, reflecting the growing willingness of various courts to intervene in the adjudicatory procedures of prisons, whether conducted by the boards of visitors, or by governors.[6] Woolf recommended the end of the adjudicatory role for boards of visitors, and this was implemented in April 1992. However, the implications for governors of the reality of judicial review in the conduct of adjudications is far reaching. Martin Mogg, at the time governor of HMP Durham, raised some of these implications, when, in 1992, he commented that it was 'hard to give proper consideration to the rules of natural justice when you have 19 or 20 adjudications to get through in a morning'.[7]

5. M LEECH (1992) A Product of the System: My Life in and out of Prison, London: Victor Gollancz, p661-63.

6.. Leech's autobiography is a useful introduction to the twists and turns of the application of the law to the prison disciplinary system. A more formal account can be found in S LIVINGSTONE and T OWEN (1993), Prison law; Text and Materials, Oxford; Clarendon Press

7. Quote taken from PM QUINN, Adjudications in Prison; Custody, Care and a little less Justice, in M LEECH (ed) (1995) The Prisoners' Handbook, Oxford; Oxford University Press. This article first appeared in The Howard Journal, Volume 32, August 1993, p191.

Peter Quinn, a prison governor, was to raise more fundamental issues in relation to the concept of justice and governors' adjudications. In particular, he believed that there were institutional pressures on governors which made the exercise of natural justice within adjudications difficult, given that the 'experience of managing the prison day in and day out will make it hard to avoid bias.' Further, he believed that staff tended to view the governors as one or other extreme on the continuum from 'the prisoners friend to a staff man.' Thus,

> 'the inter-personal and inter-professional relationships between staff and staff and staff and governor, may all have their influence on the hearing. Governors may find themselves subject to formal protest raised by The Prison Officers' Association over the manner in which they have adjudicated. A governor may be swayed by the exigencies of the regime to order a particular punishment in the hope that it may have some general deterrent effect or because of some more mundane institutional reason such as that the segregation unit is full.'[8]

Clearly conducting adjudications is a major but difficult task for prison governors. However, many of the concerns raised by Quinn and others were taken into consideration by the new Prison Discipline Manual which was introduced in February 1995. This emphasised the need for the adjudicator to 'come afresh to each inquiry, to abide by the rules of natural justice and, in the case of finding of guilt, to order a punishment that is fair and proportionate in respect of the breach of discipline'.[9] In essence this effectively drew attention to the de novo principle, preventing governors from conducting an adjudication if they 'receive information or evidence (for example, details of the prisoner's defence or some relevant incriminating admissions of criminal, disciplinary or behavioural history) which makes it impossible to hear the charge afresh'.[10] The manual also makes it clear that adjudications can be challenged if they do not meet the 'legal requirements' of natural justice. As such decisions should be legal, rational, reasonable, and procedurally correct. Similarly levels of

---

8. Ibid, pp320-327, quote taken from p322.
9. See Instruction to Governors 9/1995, p1, which authorised the introduction of the Prison Discipline Manual.
10 Prison Discipline Manual (1995), p10.

punishment have to be consistent within an establishment, and as such 'governors should discuss with adjudicators on a regular basis recent offences and punishments'.[11]

Requests and complaints

Prisoners who disagree with the results of an adjudication have a variety of avenues of appeal. At the institutional level they can use the prison's request and complaint procedures, which will result in the hearing being reviewed by the area manager. If they are dissatisfied with the result they can have the Prisons Ombudsman investigate the complaint. Similarly, they could request judicial review. However, the request and complaints procedures are used for much more than legal appeals against adjudications, and are the most common, formal process for prisoners to complain about any grievance that they might have. The procedures require the prisoner to discuss his or her grievance with wing, or landing officers, and only then, if appropriate, with the prison governor. Prisoners still not satisfied can put their complaint in writing and are entitled to written, reasoned replies. Thereafter appeals can be made outside the prison.

The Prisoners' Request/Complaints Procedures Staff Manual outlines that the principles behind the request and complaint procedures are to inspire confidence in prisoners that their interests are being looked after; to promote better relations between staff and prisoners and to 'reduce tension'. Similarly, it maintains that the procedures are to 'protect the prisoner's rights to make requests or complaints'; to allow for confidential access outside the prison; and to ensure that requests and complaints are 'fully and fairly considered' in a 'timely' manner.[12]

Timeliness, in relation to replies, is clearly one way that this might be achieved, but there needs to be much more than an ability to write quickly to a schedule. Knowing something of the prisoners within the prison, being visible on the landings and at the hot plate, and understanding the changing culture of what is happening inside the prison will also promote a better climate (see Chapter 6). However, by far the most obvious way that the governor can shape this orderly climate is through personal example. It would be very difficult, for example, to insist that there are good race relations policies within the

11. Ibid, p45.
12. Prisoners' Request/Complaints Procedures Staff Manual (1990), Part 1, p1.

prison if the governor is known to tell, or collude with, racist jokes. Similarly, it would be hard to maintain standards of time-keeping for staff if the governor is known always to be late arriving at the prison or for meetings.

Occasionally governors are also charged with criminal offences; and attitudes which might have been acceptable at university, for example, in relation to the legalisation of cannabis, become more difficult to sustain when faced with an adjudication on a prisoner found in possession of a 'controlled substance'.

The justice model

The emphasis expressed in the Prison Discipline Manual that punishments at adjudications should be 'fair and proportionate' to the offence committed is a direct application of largely American views towards sentencing, which became known as the 'the justice model.'[13] There is no single formulation of the overall approach known as 'the justice model', but its impact has been widespread. Indeed, some have argued that the Woolf Inquiry and the Criminal Justice Act of 1991 'echo' this approach.[14] In essence, the justice model reflects the growing lack of faith in the idea of rehabilitation, and thus demands the end of indeterminate sentences, such as were used in borstals, and their replacement with fixed sentences. Sentencing should merely attempt to punish the offender, in proportion to the harm caused, and should not be tailored to the individual needs, however these might be formulated. What was required were fixed sentences in proportion to the harm that resulted as a consequence of the offence.

The application of this approach to prisons is particularly apparent in the state of Minnesota, under David Fogel, who was Commissioner of the Minnesota State Department of Corrections between 1971-1973. Fogel wrote that the application of the justice model to prisons would emphasise that 'a penal sanction should only mean a temporary deprivation of liberty'. In other words, that the prison executed the sentence, and did nothing more. Indeed, he went further:

13. For a general overview of the justice model see M DAVIES, H CROALL and J TYRER (1995) Criminal Justice; An Introduction to the Criminal Justice System in England and Wales, London: Longman, pp248-253.

14. Ibid, p251

'When corrections become mixed in the dismal swamp of preaching, exhorting, and treating ('resocialisation') they become dysfunctional as an agency of justice.'[15]

A prison's regime should therefore be characterised by fairness, openness, and the application of due process. The regime should not attempt any higher moral or psychological intervention, nor should it use brutality to create order or control. Any programmes for prisoners should be voluntary, and 'opportunities for self-improvement should be offered but not made a condition of freedom.' Indeed, Fogel believed that 'administrators should immediately begin to slash the budget of all such programme services not voluntarily chosen by inmates.'[16] Instead Fogel wanted greater public scrutiny of prisons; clearer and consistent rules; law libraries in all prisons; a fight against racist expressions; the end of 'foot-dragging' when answering prisoners' complaints and exposure of any poor medical provision.[17]

Clearly these principles reflected some aspects of how regimes have developed in this country, and comments about 'foot dragging' echo the desire for 'timeliness' in relation to answering prisoners' complaints, but they have not dominated totally. The Sex Offender Treatment Programme, for example, requires all prisoners to admit their guilt, and is almost a prerequisite if the prisoner wants to be considered for parole. This is hardly 'volunteerism'. Indeed, the justice model applied to prisons is predicated upon justice existing in other parts of the criminal justice system.

Miscarriages of justice

The spate of miscarriage of justice cases, such as those involving the Birmingham Six and the Guildford Four, and the subsequent establishment of the Criminal Cases Review Commission (CCRC) in 1997 to examine convictions which appear unsafe, would suggest that justice within all parts of the criminal justice system is still an ideal, rather than a practice. This is not to suggest that prisons should have some kind of 'get out' clause, but merely reinforces the need to have all parts of the criminal justice system working together. However, there

15. D FOGEL (1978) The Justice Model for Corrections, in J FREEMAN (ed) Prisons Past and Future; in commemoration of the bi-centenary of John Howard's The State of the Prisons, London; Heinemann, pp151-177.
16. Ibid, p163.
17. Ibid, pp167-168.

are very obvious ways in which the consequences of a miscarriage case impact on the Prison Service.

Vincent Hickey, for example, together with his cousin Michael, Jimmy Robinson and the late Pat Malloy, were unsafely convicted of the murder of Carl Bridgewater. They were released from prison in February 1997, having spent 18 years in custody. Writing about his experiences Vincent Hickey maintained that 'they pulled every stroke in the book to keep us in prison. They'd lied and lied.'[18] Given the nature of their alleged offence, Hickey also claims that:

> 'In the middle of the night my cell door used to fly open and drunken screws would burst in and beat me. Then they pissed on me. I'd be fast asleep, the next thing I know my face has hit the floor ... The thing that gets to me most is the fact that they pissed on me; the lack of dignity.'[19]

Managing people who claim, and in the case of Vincent Hickey are eventually proved, to be not guilty is difficult. At one level there are security issues to take into consideration with prisoners who clearly will want to campaign to gain their freedom. Vincent and Michael Hickey, for example, took part in a rooftop protest at HMP Long Lartin, which lasted from 26 February to 20 March in 1983. Michael Hickey subsequently took part in a roof-top protest at HMP Gartree which lasted for 89 days. A long-term prison's regime is also based on the presumption that the prisoner is guilty of the crime for which he or she was convicted. A failure to acknowledge this guilt could have adverse consequences for the prisoner in relation to parole, classification, or allocation. Similarly staff working with prisoners who maintain their innocence can often have their confidence in the criminal justice system shaken, but more often than not they will simply choose not to believe the prisoner.

The concept of justice should be at the very heart of everything which prison governors do. Given their authority and their unique position within the prison, every opportunity should be taken to reinforce this message.

---

18. Vincent Hickey 'I don't have the luxury of guilt' in The Observer,, 17 August 1997. For an outline of their case, which was essentially accurate, despite being published 11 years before their release, see P FOOT Murder at the Farm; Who killed Carl Bridgewater? Harmondsworth, Penguin, 1986.

19. Ibid.

However this approach is becoming more and more difficult to sustain. On 27 November 1997, for example, more than 60 prisoners at HMPs Frankland, Long Lartin, Durham, Gartree and Maidstone went on hunger strike to highlight the number of alleged miscarriage of justice cases within the criminal justice system. CCRC receives new cases at the rate of five per day. And whilst it is difficult to establish a definitive number of prisoners who are alleging to be wrongly convicted at any one time - nor is it possible to establish how many of those who allege to be innocent are in fact eventually proven to be innocent, there is some evidence to suggest that around two per cent of the prison population might be innocent of the crimes for which they were convicted.[20]

Prison and the law[21]

Increasingly as prisoners become dissatisfied with internal procedures to alleviate their grievances, and as the law - especially the European Court of Human Rights - begins to see the work of prison as within the scope of its influence, governors have had to become mindful that decisions that they make inside can be challenged outside in the courts. The law relating to prisoners and prison is simple, at least in terms of legal theory. Primary legislation is the Prison Act of 1952, and secondary legislation is in the Prison Rules of 1999 and the Young Offender Institution Rules 1988 (as amended).

Lord Denning, in *Becker v Home Office (1972)* argued that if courts were to 'entertain actions by disgruntled prisoners that the governor's life would be made intolerable.[22] However, *Golder v UK (1975)* decided that prisoners who wanted to complain to their solicitors about their treatment in prison did not have to be subject to 'prior ventilation.'[23] 'Prior ventilation' was the requirement that prisoners must have raised a matter that they wished to complain about within the prison itself and received a definite reply to their complaint before they could raise that matter externally. The European Court of Human Rights ruled that this

20. See E CULLEN, T NEWELL (1998) Murders and Life Imprisonment - Containment, Treatment, Safety and Risk, Winchester; Waterside Press, pp55-72.

21. What follows is a very basic introduction to an increasingly important area of prison life. For those who want a full account they should see S LIVINGSTONE, T OWEN (1999) Prison Law; Text and Materials, Oxford; Clarendon Press. For an account of how the law influenced decisions in the release of one life sentenced prisoner see A ALEXANDROVICH, D WILSON (1999) The Longest Injustice: The Strange Story of Alex Alexandrovich, Winchester; Waterside Press.

22. All quotes and cases cited are taken from LIVINGSTONE AND OWEN, op cit.

23. Golder v UK (1975) 1 EHRR 524, Series A, No. 18.

violated Article 6 of the European Convention on Human Rights - the right of access to the courts. It also ruled that Mr Golder had been stopped by the prison from contacting his solicitor, which was in itself in violation of Article 8 of the Convention - the right to respect of correspondence.

Thus, gradually English courts have intervened to determine the precise nature of a prisoner's rights and entitlements. The two landmark English cases were the decision of the Court of Appeal in 1979 in *R v Board of Visitors of Hull Prison ex parte St Germain*, and in 1983 in *Raymond v Honey*.[24] This latter case arose out of a dispute when a prison governor - Colin Honey - stopped a letter from a prisoner being sent to his solicitor. The House of Lords ruled that prisoners retain all their civil rights that are not taken from them either expressly of by necessary implication.

However with the numbers of discretionary and mandatory life sentenced prisoners held in this country it was not going to take long before the European Court of Human Rights began to take an active interest in their circumstances, and indeed we owe the existence of Discretionary Life Panels (DLPs) to decisions taken in relation to the case of Robert Weeks. Mr Weeks had been sentenced to life imprisonment at the age of 17 in 1966, after he had pleaded guilty to an armed robbery. Weeks had entered the shop with a starting pistol loaded with blanks, threatened the shopkeeper, and robbed him of 35 pence. He then telephoned the police to give himself up. When they arrived he took the starting pistol out of his pocket and it went off, although no one was injured. He was released on licence for the first time in 1976, but was recalled to prison a year later and thereafter was subsequently re-released and again re-detained several times between 1977 and 1986.

The European Court of Human Rights upheld Mr Weeks' claim that on his recall to prison in 1977, and at reasonable intervals throughout his detention, he had not been able to challenge that imprisonment within the requirements of Article 5 (4) of the European Convention on Human Rights. This states that 'everyone who is deprived of his liberty by arrest or detention shall be entitled to take proceedings by which the lawfulness of his detention shall be decided speedily by a court and his release ordered if the detention is not lawful.' The court took the view that a discretionary life sentence was

24. 1979 1WLR 1401; 1983 1AC1.

not simply about punishment, but also about the protection of others, and the rehabilitation of the offender. Given that the circumstances of a person serving such a sentence would change over time, it was their legal entitlement to have their case regularly reviewed by a 'court'. The European Court of Human Rights ruled that the Parole Board did not constitute as a court, given that it had only advisory functions, and was therefore not able to order a prisoner's release. And whilst the Weeks judgement did not in itself change the procedures for reviewing the detention of discretionary lifers, it paved the way for the changes that were to be introduced by the Criminal Justice Act 1991 - in particular DLPs.

Human Rights Act 1998

The Human Rights Act comes fully into force on 2 October 2000. It makes the protections of the European Convention on Human Rights (ECHR) a part of domestic law. When the Act is in force, all public authorities including the Prison Service, will have to act compatibly with the Convention rights. The courts too will have to interpret legislation compatibly with the Convention. In addition to the Prison Service, the Board of Visitors, Parole Board and private contractors who do work on behalf of the Prison Service are classed as public authorities.

From 2 October 2000 any prisoner will be able to seek action through the UK courts on ECHR issues. The court will be able to decide whether the prisoner's individual treatment or the wider policy on which it is based, comply with the provisions of ECHR. While many Prison Service policies were shaped by the Convention others will need renewing. In the longer term case law will develop in this area and Prison Service policies and procedures will require changing. The overall impact of the Act is unknown at the time of writing but some commentators believe the Act will result in fundamental changes to prisoners' entitlements, privileges and rights.[25]

As all of this indicates, the concept of justice should be at the heart of everything governors do, not because there is increasing legal oversight of the running and management of prisons, but because they have power, authority, and a unique position within the prison which requires them to govern with fairness and equity.

25. D CHENEY, L DICKSON, J FITZPATRICK, S UGLOW (1999) Criminal Justice and Human Rights Act, Bristol, Jordan Publishing - Chapter 6 of the book deals with prisoners' rights.

CHAPTER 8

THE EXTERNAL ENVIRONMENT

> 'The message is simple — more openness leads to a better understanding and less damaging headlines.'[1]

Prisons do not exist in a vacuum. They are a very prominent part of their local communities from where, increasingly, staff are recruited. They, in turn, buy housing and household goods; send their children to local schools; drink in the town's public houses; and support the local football team. Having a prison in the town has many advantages for local businesses and others — a phenomenon perhaps best recognised in the United States, where communities compete with each other to attract prisons — but this is rarely acknowledged in Britain. Nick Flynn, for example, Deputy Director of the Prison Reform Trust, described a visit to Onley in Warwickshire, where he was invited to speak to the Residents' Association who were opposing the building of a new prison:

> 'The residents of Onley may generally support tougher law and order policies, but they do not want new prisons built in their back yard ... throughout the course of the meeting, one by one, they stood up to voice their concerns ... there will be noise pollution, traffic congestion ... farmland and endangered species of wildlife will be destroyed ... outsiders will move in to take any new jobs on offer ... house prices will increase ... school class sizes will increase ... council taxes will increase, because more police, ambulance and fire services will be needed.'[2]

Prisons clearly exert great passions among those who discuss them, or have responsibility for them. Thus, at the very least, prison governors need to acknowledge this environment so as to be more able to participate within it, help re-define it, and promote common cause and understanding. There is a variety of watchdogs and pressure groups

1. H MILLS (1996) Prison Culture, Prison Journal, No. 108, p36.
2. N FLYNN, Only the Lonely, in Prison Report: The Prison Reform Trust Magazine, No. 39, Summer 1997, pp4-5.

who monitor what goes on inside, or try to shape events. Boards of visitors, for example, made up of voluntary lay members from the community, have limited executive powers, but are appointed to satisfy themselves in relation to the administration of the prison, and the treatment of prisoners.

Pressure groups

The Prisoners' Information Book, a co-production by the Prison Service and the Prison Reform Trust, lists 51 organisations and special interest groups which are involved with prisoners or their families. These range from POPS — the Partners of Prisoners and Families Support Group — who offer advice, information, and support to those who have a loved one in prison, to GRIP — Gay Rights in Prison — who represent the interests of gay, lesbian, and bisexual prisoners and their families.[3] There are also several groups dealing solely with women, such as Women in Prison and Women's Link, and other specialist groups which deal with women who are Nigerian nationals, Jamaican or Latin American.

The four most influential external prison pressure or special interest groups or service groups are The New Bridge, the Howard League for Penal Reform, NACRO — the National Association for the Care and Resettlement of Offenders and the Prison Reform Trust. This influence stems not only from the advice and range of services which they provide but also from the fact that they campaign, to a lesser or greater degree, on behalf of prisoners — thus influencing the wider political debate — and participate with Home Office officials on a variety of committees and working parties. They also provide a range of information for prisoners, which again helps to shape and stimulate the debate which goes on inside a prison. For example, The New Bridge has produced *'Inside Time'*, a quarterly newspaper for prisoners, since 1990. It is distributed free to all prisons. In 1995 the paper had 1,056 letters and 85 articles from prisoners submitted for publication, which is some measure of its popularity, and interviews with such people as the Archbishop of Canterbury and the Chairman of the POA.[4]

The New Bridge was founded in 1956 to create links between the offender and the community. It seeks to achieve this objective by

3. The Prisoners' Information Book is an excellent source document aimed at prisoners about their time inside. The last edition was in 1999, and the various organisations mentioned are described in the book.

4. The New Bridge Annual Report, 1995, p10.

befriending people in prison through its own national network of voluntary associates (VAs), who will write to offenders and visit them in prison. The VAs are regionally based, and in 1996, for example, the Greater London area had 268 VAs who had befriended more than 1000 prisoners. It also employs four employment officers and runs an employment service for ex-offenders. They were able to find 324 ex-offenders jobs or training places in 1995, a considerable achievement given the state of the job market. The New Bridge also sponsors Family Matters courses in six prisons, aimed at helping those prisoners with children, or those planning to have children, to become more aware of the nature of family life, and the role and responsibilities of parenthood. Similarly, it runs annual youth conferences, to increase awareness about issues relating to the criminal justice system.

The Howard League is the oldest of the penal pressure groups, and is named in honour of John Howard, the reforming eighteenth century High Sheriff of Bedford who visited and wrote about prisons in England and Wales, and who died in 1790. In 1866 the Howard Association was formed in his memory, aimed at promoting 'a reformatory and radically preventative (sic) treatment of offenders', which in 1921 joined forces with The Penal Reform League to become The Howard League for Penal Reform.[5] In essence The Howard League for Penal Reform is a researching and campaigning organisation committed to reforming the criminal justice and penal system. It is funded entirely from donations, enjoys a national and international reputation, and has United Nations consultative status. It has been particularly successful at campaigning on behalf of young offenders, especially in relation to preventing suicides in prison. Their trouble-shooter project was launched in 1993, aimed at securing the release of 15 year-olds from custody and finding them alternative placements. In 1996 they sponsored a series of trouble-shooter workshops in prisons which held 15 year-olds, launching the series at HMYOI Feltham, which had had a number of suicides,[6] to encourage debate between the different agencies involved with young people in trouble. The Howard League for Penal Reform also sponsors various lecture programmes, has an annual media award, sponsors the *Howard Journal of Criminal*

5. For a short introduction to the history of The Howard League for Penal Reform see S SHERRATT, John Howard and the Howard League, in A Tribute to John Howard: The Howard League for Penal Reform, 1990, pp4-8.

6. The Howard League Annual Report 1995/96, London: The Howard League for Penal Reform, pp16-17.

Justice, and *Criminal Justice Matters*. The former publication is extremely influential, is published quarterly by Blackwells, and is regarded as one of the most important criminology journals in the country. By 1996 the journal had 382 institutional subscribers, 99 of whom were in North America, and 64 in Europe, and was marketed at virtually every major criminology conference in Britain and Europe. Its Editorial Advisory Group has leading academics, policy makers, and criminal justice practitioners on its board, reinforcing links between theory and practice, and thus pushing forward debate.

NACRO was founded in 1966, with its origins in the former National Association of Discharged Prisoners' Aid Societies. It aims to prevent crime, and to promote the re-settlement of offenders into the community. It is the largest of the four pressure groups described here, employing over 1,000 staff based in almost 150 offices and projects, spread throughout England and Wales. As such it is much more than a pressure group and a registered charity. It has, for example, a registered Housing Association, and its trading activities are managed through NACRO Trading Ltd. Whilst it receives charitable donations, NACRO is also funded by grants and contracts from government departments and agencies, local authorities, and Training and Enterprise Councils (TECs). As such it seeks to provide accommodation; runs training schemes; provides a resettlement service in a variety of prisons; and manages the Prison Link unit which by 1995 had trained its 1000th prison officer to give advice on housing and employment to prisoners approaching release.[7]

All of these activities have had their problems. For example, on their 25th anniversary in 1991 their Annual Report drew attention to the severe cutbacks that NACRO experienced since the creation of TECs, which resulted in it having to negotiate for funding with 83 separate bodies instead of centrally. This reduced their funding significantly, saw over 500 staff being made redundant, and a reduction of their training schemes from 126 to just 43.[8] This is also indicative of the wider problem that pressure groups have when they accept government subsidies, which inevitably makes it more difficult to criticise the government which has supplied that subsidy. Some of these difficulties are overcome through channelling comment about penal policy through the Penal Affairs Consortium, which was established in late 1988, at the

7. NACRO, Annual Report, 1994-95, London: NACRO, p15.
8. NACRO, Annual Report, 1990-91, London: NACRO, p8.

suggestion of Baroness Ewart-Biggs, and which has been chaired from its inception by Paul Cavadino of NACRO.

The Prison Reform Trust (PRT) is the newest, and the smallest of the organisations described, founded in 1981, and chaired at that time by Sir Monty Finniston. Now under the chairmanship of Lord Hurd of Westwell, a former Home Secretary, it published its new manifesto for penal reform in April 1997 calling for a new Prison Act and a variety of specific reforms related to the running or administration of prisons. These included the setting up of a 'second' HMP Grendon; an increase in the number of resettlement prisons; a review of the Prison Service's incentives and earned privileges policy; the abolition of the body-belt and the installation of in-cell television. Its 'guiding principles' are that the criminal justice system plays only a limited role in controlling the incidence and seriousness of crime; that imprisonment will do little to affect the rate of offending and thus that there should be a greater emphasis on community penalties.[9]

As is obvious from this very short description of their new manifesto, the PRT is the most radical of these four groups and, arguably, the most effective at influencing politicians and the public. This is achieved by its ability to research and brief journalists and others on issues affecting prisons, its various publications, and a willingness to debate issues of the day on radio and television. The BBC Home Affairs Correspondent Jon Silverman, for example, commented that 'many journalists turn to the Prison Reform Trust or the Howard League for insights into the prison system rather than the Service itself.'[10] The PRT holds an Annual Lecture, which in 1997 was delivered by Lord Bingham, the Lord Chief Justice of England, and in 1998 by Jack Straw — the new Home Secretary. It produces the Prisoners' Information Book, together with the Prison Service; runs a national penfriend scheme with around 850 members of the public writing to people in custody; and deals with numerous queries of prisoners and their families in relation to their sentence. It also publishes a list of 'achieving prisons', drawing attention to those prisons which in the PRT's view are examples of 'best practice'. These have included HMPs Grendon and Woodhill, and HMYOI Lancaster Farms.

9. A New Programme for Prison Reform, London: The Prison Reform Trust.

10. J SILVERMAN, Get Real: The Public Image of the Prison Service, Prison Service Journal No 112, July 1997, pp10-11.

HM Chief Inspector of Prisons and the Prisons Ombudsman

The origins of the modern Inspectorate lie in the 1979 May Committee.[11] Until this time inspections had been undertaken by the Inspectorate of the Prison Department headed by the Chief Inspector of the Prison Service, who was a member of the Prisons Board. Inspections were thus almost a management task, with very limited terms of reference, whose findings were then presented to the Prisons Board itself.

The May Inquiry recommended that there should be an Inspectorate independent of the Prisons Board, with much greater openness, so as to provide an authoritative check on the work done by the Prison Service on behalf of the public. As such May recommended that the Chief Inspector should be a Crown appointment, answering directly to the Home Secretary, and that the reports of inspections should be published. W H Pearce, the former Chief Probation Officer of Inner London, became the first HM Chief Inspector of Prisons in 1981, and HMP Featherstone was the first prison inspected in January of that year. The first annual report of the new Inspectorate drew attention to three areas of concern 'with which we were less than happy', and these related to overcrowding, the time that inmates spent locked in their cells, and the maintenance of the prison estate.[12]

The first Chief Inspector died in 1982, to be replaced by Sir James Hennessy, who served until 1987, when Judge Stephen Tumim, perhaps the most controversial of all Chief Inspectors, took control. Tumim's difficulties related partly to the agenda he wanted to set and partly to his high media profile. However, all of this became exacerbated when the penal debate became dominated by a philosophy characterised by the view that 'prison works'. It was clear that he did not share this view, and as a consequence his relationship with Michael Howard often appeared strained. The annual report of 1994-1995, for example, asked for 'sympathetic monitoring and a supportive approach' from ministers.[13] Whether or not he got what he asked for is for others to decide, but the agenda set by Tumim, and a series of able Deputy Chief Inspectors, demanded the introduction of in-cell sanitation; the end of

11. Committee of Inquiry into the United Kingdom Prison Services (May Report) (1979), London: HMSO, See, especially, pp92-96 and p279

12. Report of Her Majesty's Chief Inspector of Prisons for England and Wales (1981), London: HMSO, p11.

13. Report of HM Chief Inspector of Prisons for England and Wales, April 1994 — March 1995, London: HMSO, pxiii.

'slopping out'; the end of 'trebling' in one cell and the provision of constructive regimes inside. Very much in opposition to the idea that 'prison works', Tumim wanted 'the majority' of prisons to operate as pre-release centres, with 'useful, positive occupations', and rhetorically asked of young men remanded in custody 'What is the use of prison for them?'[14] Tumim also published a series of 'thematic reviews', including one on suicide prevention. Sir David Ramsbotham, the current Chief Inspector, has used this technique in relation to the incarceration of women, young offenders and suicide.

In the opening paragraphs of the first Chief Inspector's annual report he made it clear that he was 'not a Prisons Ombudsman', and as such was specifically 'excluded from investigating individual grievances'.[15] The Prisons Ombudsman was not appointed until 1994, as a result of recommendations made in the Report of the Woolf Inquiry. Woolf wanted an 'a venue of appeal to an independent person', so as to give the grievance procedure 'a validity which it does not otherwise have'.[16] The first Prisons Ombudsman was Sir Peter Woodhead, formerly the naval Deputy Supreme Allied Commander in the Atlantic, whose office began receiving complaints in October 1994. Symbolically he chose to find office accommodation outside of Prison Service Headquarters. The current Ombudsman is Stephen Shaw, who previously had been Director of the Prison Reform Trust.

The purpose of the Prisons Ombudsman is to provide an independent point of appeal for prisoners who remain dissatisfied after pursuing a complaint through the internal request and complaints system. The Prisons Ombudsman can investigate any action taken by the Prison Service which affects an individual prisoner, except for clinical complaints against medical staff or any complaint which is subject to legal proceedings. The Prisons Ombudsman's remit includes complaints about the operation of contracted out prisons and services and the actions of people working in prisons, such as probation officers, but who are not employed by the Prison Service. He can make recommendations only, and thus cannot make executive decisions. Nor can the Prisons Ombudsman investigate any decision taken personally by a Minister. Nonetheless, in his first annual report, Woodhead

14. Ibid, pxvi.

15. Report of Her Majesty's Chief Inspector of Prisons for England and Wales (1981), London: HMSO, p3.

16. Prison Disturbances April 1990 — Report of an Inquiry (Woolf Report) (1991), London: HMSO, pp418-419.

commented that he felt that he had made 'a significant contribution not just to the resolution of individual problems but also to a fairer and more just prison system'.[17] During the first year of its operation the Prisons Ombudsman received 2,050 complaints, of which 424 were investigated, and 44 per cent were upheld. Most of the complaints received during this first year related to the handling of prisoners' property; adjudications; temporary release and transfer and categorisation.

The media

Most governors, at some stage in their career, will have to deal with the media. Usually this will involve inviting a journalist from the local press into the prison to cover a story related to the prison's charity work, but on other occasions, especially after a serious disturbance or a suicide, there will be national media demanding statements and press conferences at the prison's gate. 'The plain fact is that prisons', according to Heather Mills, formerly Home Affairs Editor at The Independent and The Observer, 'are a constant source of good copy'.[18] Mills acknowledged, as most governors would have pointed out, 'escapes, riots, drugs, sex and notorious offenders like Myra Hindley, Rosemary West, and Peter Sutcliffe are always going to grab headlines', from other images of the work done inside the prison.[19]

Given all of this, governors might be forgiven for believing that the best way to deal with the press is to ignore them. However, Jon Silverman believes that this sheltering 'behind corporate walls, hoping that the storm will leave them unscathed' is unrealistic. Instead he suggests that governors should 'let more daylight in', in the shape of journalists, and that governors should be given their head to explain what they do, as he has found them 'on the whole ... some of the more impressive public servants handicapped by one of the least impressive images'.[20] This view accords with that of Mills, who cited the initiative taken by Andrew Coyle, when he was governor of HMP Brixton, in inviting the press in to see what he was attempting to do.

> 'Contrast that with the way Andrew Coyle handled the disasters that hit Brixton in the 1980s — its notorious

17. Prisons Ombusdman — Annual Report 1995, London: Prisons Ombusdsman, p1.
18. H MILLS, Prison Culture, Prison Service Journal, November 1996, No. 108, pp34-36.
19. Ibid p35.
20. Ibid p11.

> psychiatric F wing and the escape of two IRA men, made it as bad as the Whitemoor, Parkhurst and Holloway of today. He invited the media in to see for themselves the difficulties Brixton was facing and explained how he was dealing with them. He got a fairly sympathetic ride and Brixton rarely makes the news these days.'[21]

The Prison Service has attempted to counteract the generally negative publicity which prisons generate by co-operating, for example, with Channel 4's *'Banged Up'* season in May 1997. This saw access being given to the media to make programmes on such issues as the work of drugs dogs at HMP Preston and the filming of the chef, Anthony Worrall-Thompson, who was invited to cook the prison meal at HMP Wymott. Whether or not this openness continues remains to be seen, but the challenge for governors is, in the words of Silverman, to 'get real', end the culture of 'secrecy and defensiveness, and instead to develop the same type of relationship which journalists have with the police.'[22]

Where does all of this leave the governor? Clearly there are many people, groups, or organisations, both inside the Prison Service and external to it, who retain an interest in the work of the prison. Some will have statutory powers, whilst others will simply have a campaigning role about aspects of its operation. All of this merely adds to the complexity described in the area manager review. Ultimately, it is for the governor to determine the best way to make this complexity manageable, and increasingly this is to recognise that the community outside the prison's walls has as many legitimate needs and interests in the prison's work as those on the inside.

---

21. Ibid p36.
22. Ibid p11.

CHAPTER 9

SETTING STANDARDS AND MEASURING ACHIEVEMENT

> 'Performance indicator systems are potentially oscillatory - instead of steady improvement they may wobble between vulnerable simplicity and unintelligible complexity.'[1]

During recent years prison governors, like their public sector counterparts elsewhere, have been faced with demands to set clear standards and to create indicators to measure performance. Yet the move to indicator driven management, based on the creation of performance measures, has not always led to performance improvement in the public sector. The Prison Service is subject to a number of international standards but has also created its own set of operating standards. Standards have been defined as:

> 'Exemplars specifying measurable outputs or levels of service, intended to provide uniform targets and benchmarks for performance. Well-known to British industry and the professions, standard-setting has more recently spread to the service sector and, under the pressure of Government initiatives such as the Citizen's Charter, to the public services. Such standards are usually internally devised, often with some element of external validation (or accreditation) to credibly demonstrate performance.'[2]

The Prison Service was not immune from the Citizen's Charter initiative and produced a Citizen's Charter standards of service document setting out standards of service to the public, prisoners and visitors to prison.[3] A copy of the Charter is at Appendix 3.

---

1. C POLLITT (1990) Performance Indicators, Root and Branch, in M CAVE, M KOGAN and R SMITH (eds) Output and Performance Measurement in Government: The State of the Art, London: Kingsley. See for example the impact on the Magistrates court: J RAINE and M WILLSON (1997) From Performance Measurement to Management, January-March 1997, p19-25. For an account of the criminal justice system and target setting see M NASH and S SAVAGE (1995) Criminal Justice Managers: Setting targets or becoming targeted? International Journal of Public Sector Management, Vol 8, No. 1, pp4-10.
2. N NEWCOMEN (1994) Standards and Accreditation - Lessons from the USA. Prison Service Journal, May 1994, No 93, pp2-8.
3. Prison Service (1993) Citizens Charter Standards of Service, April 1993.

Performance indicators can serve a number of purposes for an organisation[4] At an institutional level performance indicators are concerned with legitimacy renewal; obtaining resources and demonstrating whether the organisation has achieved its goals. At a managerial level they provide information on individual performance and unit resource allocation, and then allow for process corrections in-year. Performance indicators also have a technical function which is concerned with effectiveness and quality of what is being performed. Like other public sector organisations the Prison Service is subject to complex auditing mechanisms to ensure that standards are met and that public money is used appropriately. These issues of setting standards, measuring performance and auditing compliance are explained in this chapter.

International standards

The United Nations, and other international bodies, have for many years, sought to set standards and promulgate rules and regulations on the detention and treatment of prisoners. The Universal Declaration of Human Rights, adopted in 1948, outlaws torture and cruel, inhuman or degrading treatment or punishment (Article 5). Since then the declaration has been joined by several other international conventions or resolutions, including the United Nations Standard Minimum Rules for the Treatment of Prisoners (SMR), adopted in 1955. The SMR deal in some detail with prison conditions and the treatment of prisoners. Whilst not an international treaty or convention, the SMR provisions are complementary to more general international conventions. In their turn the SMR have been supported, since then, by other UN instructions, which have emphasised or elaborated aspects of humanity in prison conditions and prisoners' treatment.[5] These include:

- The International Covenant on Civil and Political Rights, 1966;
- The Convention against Torture and Other Cruel Inhuman or Degrading Treatment or Punishment, 1984;

4. R KANTER and D SUMMERS (1987) Doing well, while doing good: Dilemmas of performance measurement in non profit organisations and the need for a multiple constituency approach in W POWELL (ed) The Non Profit Sector: A research handbook. Yale University Press.

5. Details of the International Standards and SMR can be found in Penal Reform International (1995) Making Standards Work: An international handbook on good prison practice, London: PRI.

- ✦ The Body of Principles for the Protection of All Persons under any form of Detention or Imprisonment, 1988;
- ✦ The Basic Principles for the Treatment of Prisoners, 1990.

The European Commission has no provisions expressly governing conditions of imprisonment. In 1973 the Council of Europe adopted the SMR. The original 94 rules which make up the SMR were never amended. In 1977 a new rule (Rule 95) was added in order to extend the scope of the SMR by explicitly including persons detained without charge. More recently, the European Prison Rules (EPR) supplemented the SMR. Like the SMR the EPR do not constitute a convention: they are not binding in law either internationally or in national systems but are intended to serve as guidelines for the organs of the convention at national administrations and courts. The Council of Europe recommends that 'governments of member states be guided in their internal legislation and practice by the principles set out in the text of the European Prison Rules ... with a view to their progressive implementation'.[6] The EPR are in four sections: the rules; an explanatory memorandum with a commentary on each rule; the historical background to the rules and a concordance of the EPR and SMR. Loucks points out that the added detail was intended to enhance understanding and improve the level of implementation'.[7] The Committee on Co-operation in Penal Affairs reported to the European Committee on Crime Problems in 1986, and the revised EPR were adopted by the Council of Europe in February 1987.

It should not be assumed that the standards in the prisons in England and Wales conform to all the international conventions and treaties to which the United Kingdom is a signatory. For example, in 1990 the Council of Europe's Committee for the Prevention of Torture found that the overcrowding in Brixton, Leeds and Wandsworth prisons, when coupled with the lack of integral sanitation and the lack of out-of cell activities, constituted 'inhuman and degrading treatment'.[8]

6. Recommendations of the Committee of Ministers to member states of the European Prison Rules - adopted 12 February 1987. A fuller explanation of the EPR is contained in N LOUCKS (ed) (1993) Prison Rules: A Working Guide, London: Prison Reform Trust.

7. Ibid, p10.

8. Council of Europe (1991) Report to the Government on the visit to the UK carried out by the European Committee of the Prevention on Torture and Inhuman or Degrading Treatment or Punishment from 29 July to 10 August 1990, Strasbourg: Council of Europe.

Minimum standards in England and Wales

The decade following the Council of Europe's adoption of the SMR in 1973 saw a growing movement advocating the introduction of minimum enforceable standards for the prisoners held in the prisons of England and Wales. The movement had, amidst its ranks, the May committee which recommended a minimum target of no enforced cell sharing, regular access to lavatories, or integral sanitation,[9] and HM Chief Inspector of Prisons who called for a code of standards of prisoners' rights which should 'ultimately be approved by Parliament'.[10] On 17 December 1982, Patrick Mayhew, Minister of State at the Home Office, in a Parliamentary reply to Robert Kilroy-Silk MP, announced his intention to produce a draft code of minimum standards for prisons during 1983. However by the end of 1983 the Home Office had not delivered its promised draft code and the commitment was officially withdrawn the following year. The fight for minimum standards was taken up by the Governors' Branch of the Society of Civil and Public Servants which, in 1983, published a set of 'Prison Standards' in a move to 'accept the responsibilities inherent in our work and take a decisive lead'.[11] In early 1984, NACRO published its own document: 'Minimum Standards for Prison Establishments'.[12] However, the response from Government was less than supportive and the new Minister of State took the view that 'we do not consider that a code of minimum standards for prisons would advance the programme the Government has in hand for improving prison conditions'.[13] The Woolf report took a different view stating:

> 'In order to achieve justice within prisons there must be required standards of conditions and regimes within prisons. After proper consultation, the Home Secretary should establish a series of National Accredited Standards applicable to all prisons. It would then be the responsibility of every prison establishment to reach at least that standard ... for the time being, the National Standards would have to be

9. Committee of Inquiry into the United Kingdom Prison Service (May Committee) 1979, Cmnd. 7673, London: HMSO.

10. Report of HM Chief Inspector of Prisons, 1982, para 5.11.

11. Prison Governors' Branch (1983) Prison Standards, Society of Civil and Public Servants, para 7.

12. S CASALE (1984) Minimum Standards for Prison Establishments, London: NACRO.

13. J PATTEN - Reply to a Parliamentary Question, Hansard 21 July 1987.

aspirational. Once they are achieved, that would be the time to consider whether it was necessary to make them legally enforceable. We would, however, expect that at that stage they would be incorporated in the Prison Rules and so would be legally enforceable by judicial review.'[14]

The Government White Paper, produced in response to Woolf, made clear that the Government intended to codify the versions of existing standards, and went on to state:

'They should be focused directly on the service to be provided for prisoners. They should cover the standard of accommodation, such as cell space, heating and lighting; the basic necessities of life, such as the provision of food and clothing and hygiene arrangements; and the access which prisoners should have to a range of regime facilities, including visits and other contacts with family members. The principal aim of the standards would be to set clear targets which all establishments would in time be expected to meet and against which the provisions in any other establishment could be judged. The Government agrees with the Woolf Report that questions relating to enshrining the standards in the Prison Rules, and to their enforceability, should be considered when the standards can be met consistently in all establishments.'[15]

A Code of Standards was finally published in April 1994, in a document entitled HM Prison Service Operating Standards.[16] The covering letter, by the Director General, to all governors made clear that 'all Prison Service establishments will aim to meet (the standards) over time' and that 'meeting the operational standards will be a line management responsibility'. The introduction to the standards document reinforced the point that governors were expected to work towards achieving the standards 'over time' and that their standards were neither intended to be legally enforceable nor to provide any

14. Prison Disturbances April 1990 (Woolf Report) (1991) Cmnd 1456, London: HMSO, para 1.186-1.187.

15. Home Office (1991) Custody, Care and Justice - The way ahead for the Prison Service in England and Wales, Cm 1947, London: HMSO, para 6.14- 6.22

16. HM Prison Service (1994) Operating Standards.

guarantee that every standard will be met in every institution at any particular time.

Standards Manual

The Prison Service Corporate Plan for 1999 - 2002 announced that new Prison Service Standards would be introduced in 1999. As a result the Prison Service Standards Manual was formally issued on 20 May 1999. It contained the first five of around sixty new standards which were to be issued periodically every two-three months over the following eighteen months. The Standards became immediately applicable on issue.

The manual made clear that the aim of issuing new Standards was:

> 'To bring about an acceptable and consistent level of service delivery by Prison Service Staff and further the achievement of the objectives set for the Prison Service.'

In developing the new Prison Service Standards it was decided that they should:

- ✦ be clear and concise, written in plain English in a consistent house style using a standard layout;
- ✦ conform to current legislation;
- ✦ be achievable and affordable across the Service;
- ✦ be measurable and auditable; and
- ✦ keep prescriptive elements to the minimum required to achieve a consistent delivery of service.

The Prison Service Standards provide the strategic context for senior managers, and all staff in the Service. The Standard sets out required practice on a specific topic and is formulated in such a way that both performance against it and compliance with it can be measured. It is aimed at all staff, not only those managers and staff involved in delivery in the area of business covered. Each standard incorporates the key baselines against which performance can be audited. It was hoped that the manual would help this process by making clear:

- ✦ what staff are expected to deliver;
- ✦ what their actions are intended to achieve; and
- ✦ how compliance will be checked.

The Standards set goals which establishments would generally be able to meet. Occasionally, an establishment is unable to meet a Standard, for example, because of resource constraints or other operational pressures. In such cases, an implementation plan is agreed with the area manager to achieve compliance within no more than three years.

Exceptionally, a specific baseline may not be appropriate to a particular prison. In that case, an alternative process to achieve the same 'required action' is agreed with the area manager and policy group.

The Prison Service Standards did not change the legal rights of individuals nor did they imply additional rights or entitlements. The audit baselines were considered as management tools to assist in managing the performance of the Prison Service in a consistent way.

A copy of the alphabetical index of all Standards is shown in Appendix 5.

Auditing Standards

The Prison Service Corporate Plan 1994-97 contained the strategic priority 'Setting standards for establishments and developing a system of performance review and audit'.[17] The plan described how the introduction of establishment business plans, supported by operating standards, provided for the first time a comprehensive benchmark of the standards the Service aimed to meet. It went on to state that the progressive implementation of these standards, supported by systems for monitoring individual establishments' performance, would be one of the Service's main priorities over the ensuing three years. One of the main 'monitoring' mechanisms was through the creation of the Standards Audit Unit (SAU). The SAU was established in November 1994 but it was quickly hijacked to perform purely security audits of the closed prison estate as one of the Prison Service's main responses to the Woodcock report into the escape of six prisoners from Whitemoor in September 1994.

It is also worth noting that, because of having to conduct security audits, the modus operandi of the SAU became one of a limited audit activity to measure compliance and management controls. The SAU has essentially been locked into this audit style ever since. In addition to auditing security the other main task of the SAU is to audit Prison

17. HM Prison Service (1994) Corporate Plan 1994-1997, para 3.1

Service strategic priorities and the standards and policies that underpin them. This work commenced in April 1996. The current terms of reference include:

- ✦ carrying out independent assessments of the degree to which establishments meet Prison Service strategic priorities and the operating standards and policies underpinning them;
- ✦ reporting findings to the Director General, operational directors, area managers and governors concerned and to award compliance ratings;
- ✦ auditing each establishment once every two years;
- ✦ identifying operating standards which require review;
- ✦ offering advice on implementing standards;
- ✦ disseminating best practice throughout the Service;
- ✦ identifying where resource deficiencies may have inhibited the achievement of an operating standard;
- ✦ identifying trends and emerging themes;
- ✦ highlighting good practice and common areas of non-compliance;
- ✦ publishing an annual report to the Prison Service Management Board.

The strategic priorities, policies and key controls underpinning audit modules have been analysed to identify key compliance baselines. The audit assumption is that if the key compliance baselines are satisfied then there is reasonable assurance that all other aspects of that particular policy are also in place. Each establishment is given an overall compliance rating at the end of either a standards or security audit. Additionally, in standards audits, each strategic priority audit module is also given a compliance rating. The Prison Service introduced compliance ratings as a means of:

- ✦ providing a clearer description of the level of compliance with core standards contained in the Manual on Security and other corporate plan strategic priorities;
- ✦ offering establishments a clearer view on their performance of important procedures and controls, enabling staff to draw reassurance from the results;
- ✦ focusing attention on improving performance where necessary, and assisting both the post-audit action plan and integrated planning processes;

- setting the baseline against which subsequent internal and external audits will be based;
- enabling accurate conclusions to be drawn about the performance of the Service as a whole and different types of establishment in particular (for example, dispersals, locals, category C, etc.); and
- setting the agenda for the Prisons Board and Executive Committee in reviewing current policy and identifying future priorities.

The rating system is based upon the judgement of the Standards Audit Team leader alone. That judgement is exercised within a publicly declared audit methodology and with the object of achieving reasonable assurance that programmes, procedures and practice are in compliance with mandatory requirements and subject to effective internal control systems.

Performance is measured against a set of publicly declared key compliance baselines for each programme, procedure or practice. Wherever possible, material evidence is gathered and evaluated against these baselines. Findings are declared as complying or not complying with the relevant baseline. Any deviations from the baselines are noted and reported under the following classification.

a. **Advised Point:** - a relatively minor yet clear non-compliance from mandatory requirements which can normally be remedied quickly and without recourse to additional resources.
b. **Deficiency:** - a serious single non-compliance or series of related 'advised' level non-compliances which, if not remedied quickly, could eventually lead to a significant failing. Some deficiencies can still be remedied quickly and without recourse to additional resources but others may be more complex and take some time and re-prioritising of work to remedy.
c. **Significant Finding:** - a significant single failure or series of related deficiencies which has or could result in important mandatory requirements not being delivered thereby placing the establishment at risk of an immediate major failing. Notwithstanding the difficulties involved, it is considered that such findings must be remedied as a top priority.

Advised points, deficiencies and significant findings are published in a written report and included in the post-audit action plan. This action plan is audited on future SAU visits to the establishment. Any findings which remain non-compliant on follow-up audit are headlined in the subsequent audit report.

The team leader considers all evidence provided by the advised, deficient and significant findings recorded and after taking other matters such as complexity or special difficulties into account, awards a compliance rating to each module that has been audited. The team leader then takes all the individual module compliance ratings into account and awards overall compliance ratings to the establishment as a whole for security, standards and action planning.

The compliance ratings are:

a. **Superior:** - an establishment, function or particular activity is performing all its work in an exceptional manner and has excellent internal controls. Non-compliances are limited in number and not serious in nature. Performance exceeds expectations and demonstrates initiative and exceptional effort.
b. **Good:** - the establishment, function or activity is performing all of its work well and there are few deficient procedures. Internal controls are such that there are limited procedural deficiencies. Overall performance is above an acceptable level.
c. **Acceptable:** - this is the baseline for the rating system. The work of the establishment, function or activity is being adequately performed. Although numerous non-compliances may exist, they do not detract from the acceptable accomplishment of mandatory work. Internal controls are such that there are no major performance breakdowns that would prevent the activity or establishment from continuing its overall objectives.
d. **Deficient:** - an unsatisfactory number of activities or key compliance baselines within them are not being performed at an acceptable level. Internal controls are weak, thus allowing for serious deficiencies in one or more activity area to develop and continue undetected or un-addressed.
e. **Unacceptable:** - an establishment, function or activity is impaired to the point that it is clearly not accomplishing the required objectives. Internal controls are not sufficient to

reasonably assure that acceptable performance can be expected in the future.

During the audit the team leader holds 'close-off' meetings with the governor and/or key members of staff at the end of each day. The team presents the good practices and non-compliances found that day and announces the modular ratings that have been awarded. Subsequently, the governor receives a written record of these findings in action plan format. Amongst other things, the purpose of the daily meeting is to enable the establishment to consider and, if necessary, challenge audit findings. The audit team always produce evidence to support their findings. The establishment can also use the meeting to advise the team of any findings which have been remedied during the course of the visit. These can be verified by the team and noted on the final report.

On the final day of the audit, the team leader holds a meeting with the governor and hands over a provisional report which contains an action plan listing all non-compliance findings. The report also highlights good practice and any 'commendations'. The governor is also given copies of the audit worksheet for each key compliance baseline not complied with. These provide more details and evidence in support of the findings and assist action planning. The governor is advised of the ratings for each audit module and the overall ratings as decided by the team leader. There are separate overall ratings for standards audit, security audit and action plan performance.

Within a further 28 days a final report is issued from the SAU in accordance with PSI 3/1997. Establishments have 28 days from receipt of the final report to submit their action plan for approval by the area manager. Audit working papers are stored in the SAU in Corby and available on request. They also have an important part to play in preparation for the next audit of the establishment.

The audit methodology applied by the SAU is based on the work of the United States Federal Bureau of Prisons Programme Review Division.[18] Their operational audit arrangements have been in place for about ten years and are accredited by the American Correctional Association. SAU have adapted and developed these procedures to

18. An overview of the approach to standards and accreditations in the USA is contained in N NEWCOMEN (1994) Standards and acceptable lessons from USA, in Prison Service Journal, May 1994, No. 93, pp2-8.

meet the needs of the Prison Service. The main features are an audit visit of 12 working days duration and an audit team of four or five people. In addition to the external SAU audit, establishments are encouraged to undertake self-auditing using SAU key compliance baselines which have been distributed to governors.[19]

Finance audit

Prison Service internal audit services (PSIAS) provide the Director General, through the audit committee, with an assurance on the adequacy and effectiveness of the internal financial control system and the extent to which it can be relied upon.[20] The PSIAS have a broad remit which covers the whole network of systems and controls established:

- to achieve corporate objectives;
- to ensure the economical and efficient use of resources;
- to ensure compliance with established policies, procedures, laws and regulations;
- to safeguard the Service's assets and interests from losses of all kinds, including those arising from fraud, irregularity and corruption ; and
- to ensure the integrity and reliability of information, accounts and data.

Governors have a personal responsibility for the propriety and regularity of the public finances for which they are answerable; for the keeping of proper accounts; for prudent and economical administration; for the avoidance of waste and extravagance; and for the efficient and effective use of all available resources. PSIAS aims to help governors discharge these duties, as sub-accounting officers, by reporting on the elements of the internal financial control system for which they are responsible. In particular, PSIAS undertakes the following audits of establishments:

- regular audits - one visit every three years to audit finance systems, staff management, asset management and

19. Prison Service Instruction 3/1997.
20. PSIAS was established in April 1994.

management information systems. The audit report assigns a 'control evaluation rating' following each visit;

- short unannounced visits - to check adherence to mandatory key financial controls and to undertake substantive testing of high risk systems;
- follow-up audits - undertaken within one year of a less than acceptable rating being given on a regular audit. At the end of the audit the establishment is assigned a revised control evaluation rating;
- special review - review of a specific area at the governor's request;
- anti-fraud audit activity - fraud investigations, unannounced visits and pre-emptive substantive testing of high risk systems.

There is clearly some overlap between the audit and monitoring bodies such as: SAU; National Audit Office; Home Office Internal Audit; PSIAS and HMCIP as well as professional audits such as Health and Safety and Education. Consideration is now rightly being given to the rationalisation and co-ordination of audit arrangements to avoid prisons constantly being occupied with audit teams. Ideally each prison should be audited by headquarters no more than once each year, alternating between Internal Audit and Standards Audit. Other audits undertaken by specialists should be timed to coincide and be integrated with Standards Audit, so that a total picture of the prison can be built up. The issue of replacing compliance auditing with output auditing should also be revisited. Focusing on compliance audits is, by its very nature, restricting the flexibility of governors to deliver agreed outputs in a more effective, efficient and economic way.

A further point of contention for governors is the lack of clarity about which operating standards are mandatory and which aspirational. In addition, numerous documents, manuals, orders and instructions contain standards. What governors need is a clear single set of achievable standards.

Key performance indicators

The creation of the Prison Service agency brought with it an attempt, for the first time, to measure the performance of the Service in a quantitative way. Each of the Service's objectives is supported by key performance indicators (KPIs), which are set out in the Prison Service

Framework Document.[21] The figures for the Prison Service performance against KPIs for 1992-1998 is at Appendix 4.

Each year the Secretary of State sets out the key targets in respect of each KPI.[22] The achievements of the Service against the targets are contained in the Annual Prison Service Report and Accounts which the Secretary of State lays before Parliament. The KPIs have received a number of criticisms since they were set. Sir John Learmont, in his review of Prison Service security, took the view that:

> 'The current set of eight KPIs ... was introduced at the time the Agency was formed and represented the first attempt to assess the 'business performance' of the Prison Service in a quantitative way. It was a laudable and important first step. KPIs are, however, management tools that need regular review. They send messages to the workforce about what is important. There were grounds for concern in a number of areas. First, the KPIs showed a strong bias towards care issues (five KPIs),to the potential detriment of custody (one KPI) and control (one KPI). Second, there were significant omissions in the areas of Headquarters staff reductions; staff development and commitment; recidivism; physical security; discipline; drugs; and suicides. The third major concern related to the way in which statistics were being collected and used. In particular, staff perceived KPIs, rightly or wrongly, as a benchmark for judgements about privatisation and were tempted to be economical with the truth when submitting returns. The Inquiry believes that KPIs must be revised. Performance indicators, as the name implies, only indicate and can never be a complete measure of the success or failure of an organisation. In principle, the establishment of performance indicators within the Service is wholeheartedly supported by the Inquiry but it is clear that at least some of those presently in use are not achieving their objective. Indeed, they may even be counterproductive, in respect of both security and conditions for inmates. The Prisons Board must not fall into the trap of managing the indicators rather than managing the organisation.

21. Prison Service (1993) Framework Document, April 1993, p5.
22. These targets are contained in the annual Prison Service Business Plan.

Although the Prisons Board has accepted that KPIs need to be constantly reviewed, the Inquiry has observed that the latest Business Plan, 1995-96, shows no change to the KPIs discussed in this report.'[23]

However, the 1995-96 Business Plan did indicate that the Service was committed to developing new indicators which might include:

'prevalence of drug misuse; level of serious assaults; an alternative measure of prison conditions to replace 'trebling'; a measure of closeness of prisoners' location to home, and a measure of the effectiveness of offending behaviour programmes.'[24]

As a result the 1996-97 Business Plan contained three new KPIs: random drug testing (the rate of positive random drug testing); completion of accredited offending behaviour programmes; and average training days per member of staff. A number of changes were also made to the definitions of some existing KPIs and two KPIs were dropped (number of prisoners with 24 hours access to sanitation and proportion of prisoners held in establishments where prisoners have the opportunity to exceed the minimum visiting entitlement).

The main changes in the most recent business plan (1999 - 2000) include new KPIs and targets on : escapes from contracted out escorts; cost per place; staff sickness; and correspondence response times. Two KPIs have been discontinued : time unlocked; and staff training. The plan explains that with the emphasis on constructive regimes designed to address offending behaviour, and the gradual introduction of 'in cell T.V.' what prisoners do when out of their cells is more relevant than how long they are unlocked.

Concern still exists amongst some governors about the general applicability of the KPIs to all prisons and the definition of some KPIs. For example, should purposeful activity not include time spent on visits? Should the KPI on offending behaviour programmes be applied to local prisons where there is a short term population? Is the drugs KPI

23. Review of Prison Service Security in England and Wales and the escape from Parkhurst Prison on 3rd January 1995 (Learmont Report) (1995), Home Office, Cm 3020, London: HMSO, pp86-87.

24. Prison Service (1995) Business Plan 1995-96, p3.

a fair indicator where prisons have a very high turnover and have a continually changing population?

Figure 10 : Objectives and Key Performance Indicators for 1999 - 2000

PRISON SERVICE OBJECTIVES

1. Protect the public by holding those committed by the courts in a safe, decent and healthy environment.

2. Reduce crime by providing constructive regimes which address offending behaviour, 'improve' educational and work skills and promote law abiding behaviour in custody and after release.

KPIs for 1999-2000

- ✦ To ensure no Cat A escapes.
- ✦ To ensure that the number of escapes from prisons, and escorts undertaken by Prison Service staff, expressed as a proportion of the prison population, is lower than 0.05 per cent.
- ✦ To ensure that the number of escapes from contracted out escorts is no more than 1 per 20,000 prisoners handled.
- ✦ To ensure that the number of positive adjudications of assault on staff, prisoners and others, expressed as a proportion of the average population, is lower than 9 per cent.
- ✦ To ensure that the rate of positive results from random drug tests is lower than 18.5 per cent.
- ✦ To ensure that the number of prisoners held two to cell designed for one, expressed as a percentage of the population, does not exceed 18 per cent.
- ✦ To ensure that the average cost per uncrowded prison place does not exceed £26,208.
- ✦ To ensure that the average cost per prisoner does not exceed £27,392.
- ✦ To ensure that average staff sickness does not exceed 12.5 working days per person.
- ✦ To ensure that 95 per cent of correspondence receives a reply within 20 days by October 1999.
- ✦ To ensure that prisoners spend on average at least 24 hours per week engaged in purposeful activity.
- ✦ To ensure that there are at least 3600 completions by prisoners of offending behaviour programmes as being effective in reducing reoffending, of which 700 should be sex offender programmes

The introduction of KPIs typified the move to 'managerialism' in the Prison Service. Sparks et al point to their supposed dual function 'both to ensure the general raising of standards of economy, efficiency and effectiveness and to provide additional incentives, responsibilities and opportunities for those lower down the organisation'. They identify a widespread concern that the penchant for measurement and uniform standards eroded the traditional moral (including reformative) commitments of institutions in favour of an exclusive concern with process.[25] Similar criticisms have been made about performance indicators in the public sector generally where few performance indicators take account of effectiveness, equity and quality.[26] Nevertheless, as Derek Lewis pointed out, 'a powerful tool for reinforcing a performance culture is measurement'. He considered that the introduction of KPI targets for each establishment 'concentrated the minds of governors' and that the publication of inter-prison comparison KPI data was even more effective for creating improved performance, despite the complaints about unfairness, lack of comparability and inaccuracy.[27] In order to ensure that the system is not manipulated, the collection of KPI data is now audited as part of the standards audit remit.

Richard Tilt, a past Director General, believed that:

> 'It is irrefutable that our performance has improved enormously over that period [1993-1996]. I think that the biggest contributor has been the establishing of key performance indicators and targets ... that has really focused people's attention on improving performance.'[28]

The Home Affairs Select Committee in its report on the management of the Prison Service took a similar view:

> 'The system of KPIs and associated targets, by providing a greater clarity and focus for management effort and individual performance, has played a successful role in recent Prison Service achievements.'[29]

A new Business Planning System for the Prison Service is due to go live in all establishments by April 2000. The new system was developed and piloted in 20 prisons, in 1998-99. The system identified the

25. R SPARKS, A BOTTOMS, W HAY (1996) Prisons and the Problem of Order, Oxford: Clarendon, p20.

26. See for example, C POLLITT (1990) Performance Indicators, root and branch, in M CABE, M KOGAN and R SMITH (eds) Output and Performance Management in Government: The state of the Art, London: Jessica Kingsley

27. D LEWIS (1997) Hidden Agendas : Politics, Law and Disorder, London : Hamish Hamilton, p79

28. Home Affairs Committee (1979) The Management of the Prison Service, 2nd report, Vol 2, Question 1319.

29. Ibid - Volume 1, para 133. A detailed discussion of the dangers of over reliance on KPIs can be found in para 134-140.

contribution of each functional group to the overall prison business plan, clearly identifying managerial responsibilities for performance. It enables a clear link to be forged between the performance plan of every member of staff and the standards and targets that have been set for their establishment.

New Service Delivery Agreements (SDA) between governors and area managers which set out a three year development plan for each establishment with agreed improvement targets are being developed. Three establishments started operating SDAs in the Yorkshire area in April 1999. A further four establishments began to operate them from October 1999, followed by nine more in April 2000. The new SDAs were designed to complement the new Business Planning System not to replace it.

An integrated approach

A model which may have some benefit to the future development of the Standards and Auditing System is the Institution Character Profile (ICP) used by the Federal Bureau of Prisons since 1990. This instrument was designed to assess the quality of work life for staff, the working and living conditions for prisoners, the stability of the institution and the nature of the professional relationships between federal officers. The spirit of ICP is captured by DiIulio:

> 'Managers are rewarded (or not) according to whether the cell blocks are clean, the inmates are safe, the classes orderly, the industries productive, the staff turnover rate low, the escape rate zero, and so on. A warden who fails to deliver these goods cannot excuse himself by reciting budget woes, crowding problems, red tape, too many 'heavies', or anything else.'[30]

The ICP includes structured interviews with 40 staff and 40 inmates, selected using a random sampling programme, a complete review of records (incident reports, grievances, union complaints, and so forth), and a systematic set of observations. The staff interview schedule has four sections: community relations, professionalism, staff morale, and communications. The inmate interview has 20 questions

30. J DiIULIO (1991) No Escape: The future of American Correction, New York: Basic Books, pp39-40.

rating accessibility to staff, staff responsiveness and maintenance of the facility, and quality of inmate programmes.

When the on-site ICP ends, qualitative and quantitative management indicator data are analysed and ICP reports written. These are detailed compilations of interview, observation, and records data. From these data an objective rating (unsatisfactory, minimally satisfactory, satisfactory, exceeds, outstanding) is given to about 60 of the institution's operations and programmes. Staff and inmates' perceptions about the performance and management style of a warden and executive staff are compiled. ICP reports have a limited distribution and no-one below the rank of warden has official access to them.[31] The operation of ICPs since 1990 appears to help maintain strong management with low cost, rapid assessment of management and dissemination of policies to prison staff.[32]

The introduction of 360^0 feedback from staff and prisoners on the effectiveness of governors and the perceived quality of the prison itself would be an interesting innovation in our Prison Service, but might encounter resistance from a number of powerful stakeholders.

31. For a full account of the ICP see M FLEISCHER (1996) Management assessment and Policy dissemination in Federal Prisons, in Prison Journal, Vol 76, March 1996, pp81-91, Sage.

32. Op cit, p89.

CHAPTER 10

WELL GOVERNED PRISONS

> 'Poor prison and jail conditions are produced by poor prison and jail management; cruel and unusual conditions are the product of failed management.'[1]

> 'There is nothing magical about running prisons; that said, the task is far from being a simple one. It is my firm belief that liberated management, that is to say, management unencumbered by outmoded, unproductive, unenlightened and constrictive practices, will show that prisons are no less likely to be 'successful' than any other organisation.'[2]

Achieving targets set for key performance indicators does not create a good prison. As Richard Tilt pointed out to the Home Affairs Select Committee:

> 'You can walk around a prison that is doing well in performance indicators, but which, actually, you are not very happy about.'[3]

What then are the tell-tale signs of a good, well governed prison and how were they achieved? Derek Lewis suggests that well run establishments are where 'prison officers are confident and happy to talk, where 'prisoners look you in the eye and where a governor has a grip on what is happening in his prison, knows the staff as he walks around, and has a clear sense of what he is trying to do'.[4]

A very valuable contribution to the debate about what makes a good prison was made by Sir David Ramsbotham, HM Chief Inspector of Prisons, in his thematic report on suicides: 'Suicide is everyone's concern' published in May 1999. Ramsbotham developed the idea of a good prison as being 'healthy'.

---

1. J DiLULIO (1991) No escape: The future of American Corrections, New York: Basic Books, p12
2. C ERICKSON (1992) A report on the development and principles of direct supervision in American Prisons, p3. Prison Service Library.
3. Home Affairs Select Committee (1997) The Management of the Prison Service, Vol 2, Question 146, London: HMSO.
4. D LEWIS (1997) Hidden Agendas: Politics, Law and Disorder, London: Hamish Hamilton, p48.

The concept of a healthy prison is underpinned by four main principles which can be used as tests for the health of a prison: the weakest prisoners feel safe; all prisoners are treated with respect as individuals; all prisoners are busily occupied, are expected to improve themselves and given the opportunity to do so; and all prisoners can strengthen links with their families and prepare for release. Each of these principles can be broken down into key elements for assessing a prison.

A safe prison must at least: create a safe and predictable environment; regularly monitor the well-being of prisoners to establish that they are safe; have an effective anti-bullying strategy; have an incentive anti-bullying strategy that encourages responsible behaviour and does not just reward conformity; have rules which are necessary, that are explained to prisoners and are fairly administered; keep good records of individual prisoners.

In an establishment which demonstrates respect: governors and senior managers monitor if prisoners are treated with respect through talking to them; prisoners understand how to access services, maintain family links and receive attention when in need; prisoners are approached by staff who check on their well-being and offer support; prisoners are spoken to by staff with courtesy and treated with fairness and openness; prisoners have access to a health care service equivalent to the National Health Service; prisoners receive individual attention through a recognised key worker scheme supported with training and ongoing supervision; prisoners have rights of access to appeal against decisions.

A prison providing purposeful activity will at least: ensure that all prisoners are purposefully occupied in constructive activity as part of each working day; provide a range of meaningful activities allowing for some choice where possible; encourage prisoners to understand, join in and complete programmes; allow prisoners to improve their basic literacy and numeracy skills; recognise the need to allow prisoners to achieve qualifications.

To assist resettlement, prisons will at least: challenge offending behaviour for sentenced prisoners and provide programmes to help; prevent reoffending on release; provide resettlement programmes to prepare all prisoners for release; ensure that all staff and the culture of the establishment support offending behaviour work; ensure that other statutory, voluntary or community agencies, social services and health services are involved where necessary to provide care after release; take measures to increase the employability of offenders; ensure all prisoners are released to suitable accommodation.

The role of the governor in creating and shaping a good prison is critical. An exploratory study of correctional institutions in three US states found that 'prison management may be the single most important determinant of the quality of prison life',[5] a view that would be shared by most governors in this country. Bad prisons are not inevitable; neither, though, are good prisons. To govern a prison well requires certain attributes. The common theme in good prisons, according to Lewis, is a governor with the 'vision, enthusiasm, courage, leadership and managerial skills to seize the opportunity and refuse to take no for an answer from the bureaucrats, the POA or anyone else'.[6]

Being a good governor is more than just being a good manager because, where controls and order break down, the command ability of the governor is as important as his or her managerial ability in their day to day operation. American research indicates that 'the way in which prison administrators prepare for and handle this type of crisis can make the difference between a small-scale disturbance and a fully-fledged riot'. But even contingency planning is a delicate balance in prisons as the same researchers discovered:

> 'Preparation and planning are often considered to be essential for adequate crisis management, but in the context of a penal institution some delicate choices have to be made. A tension exists between the managerial style and administrative measures required for the daily functioning of a prison and those that are employed in the preparation for low-chance events. An exaggerated emphasis on preparedness may increase feelings of insecurity among correctional personnel and may have negative repercussions for the atmosphere in the institution. An over-reliance on crisis planning could lead to unintended consequences; it may be conducive to a situation in which inmate rebellion becomes more likely.'[7]

This chapter explores various practical approaches to governing and suggests possible ways to ensure that prisons meet the Prison

5. J DiIULIO (1987) Governing Prisons, New York: The Free Press, p255.
6. D LEWIS op cit.
7. R BOIN and M Van DUIN (1995) Prison riots as organisational failures: A Management Perspective, in Prison Journal, Vol 75, No 3, September 1995, pp357-379, Sage.

Service's Purpose and Objectives. Governing requires effective leadership, the ability to act in a command role at short notice, general managerial skills and the ability to achieve balance between custody, care and justice. The key importance of leadership was reiterated in the Learmont Report:

> 'Security will remain absolutely dependent on the personal efforts of prison staff. They have a very difficult job which can be lonely, frightening or boring ... more important still [than training] is visible leadership which recognises the human dimensions, shows enthusiasm for people's efforts and promotes feelings of self respect and self confidence.'[8]

The American perspective on governing

The majority of American literature focuses on the nature and dynamics of prisoners in custody. Recently some attempts have been made to study correctional officers and to survey wardens' backgrounds and perceived administrative problems. Only two major texts have considered, in detail, the contribution and impact of wardens' correctional orientation, management style and approach to the job.

The first study, conducted by DiIulio in the 1980s, concluded that wardens' managerial style was the most salient determinant of whether prisons were safe, orderly, clean and capable of providing inmate amenities.[9] The quality of institutional life in each system was measured using three criteria: order; amenity and service. Order was defined as the absence of individual or group misconduct that threatened the safety of others (such as rates of assaults, murders, riots). Amenity was described as the availability of things that enhanced the comfort of the prisoners (good food, clean cells, decent recreational equipment). The definition of service focused on the availability of things that may improve prisoners' life prospects (offending behaviour programmes, educational or vocational training). In addition to archival research DiIulio undertook participant observation of leadership and management practices in each system. His conclusions were unequivocal and have proved somewhat controversial:

8. Review of Prison Service Security in England and Wales (Learmont Report) (1995), paras 4.39 and 4.41, London: HMSO.

9. J DiIULIO (1987) op cit, p255.

> 'I found strong, politically astute leadership, an organisational culture built around 'security-first' goals, and a paramilitary organisational structure were associated with higher levels of order, amenity, and service behind bars. Other things being equal, prisons administered along these lines did better even when they were more crowded, spent less, had fewer staff, had a more diverse racial mix, suffered more from architectural limitations, and so on, than prisons that had empty beds, spent buckets of money, had wall-to-wall staff, were more homogenous racially, and boasted state-of-the-art physical plants.'[10]

The book left open the crucial question of what types of prison leadership and management style worked best under what conditions. DiIulio has accepted that his incantation of 'security first' goals and 'paramilitary organisational structure' may apply only to high security prisons:

> 'Where lighter classes of offenders housed in duly classified low custody institutions are concerned, it is entirely in accord with common sense to suspect that less security driven regimes work as well if not better than tighter ones, both in terms of institutional outcomes (level of order, amenity and service) and in terms of prospects for reducing recidivism rates.'[11]

DiIulio felt able to identify four common characteristics found in successful prison wardens:

> 'First, successful prison directors and institutional managers are not here today, gone tomorrow. They are in office long enough to learn the job, make plans, and implement them.
> Second, they are highly 'hands on' and proactive. They pay close attention to details and do not wait for problems to arise but attempt to anticipate them. While they trust their subordinates and do their share of paperwork, they keep

10. J DiULIO (1991) Understanding Prisons: The new old penology in Law and Social Inquiry, Vol 16, pp65-99, American Bar Foundation, p82.
11. Ibid p85.

themselves focused on the prisons and what is actually happening inside of them. At the same time, they recognise the need for outside support.

Third, they act consciously to project an image of themselves that is appealing to a wide range of people from inside and outside of the organisation. Fourth, they are dedicated and fiercely loyal to the department and see themselves as keepers engaged in a noble and challenging (if mostly thankless) profession.'[12]

The debate in the USA was taken a step further with the publication, in 1994, of Kevin Wright's book entitled 'Effective Prison Leadership'. Wright's book is very much a 'how-to book'. It describes how prison officials should do their jobs, what actions they should take, what they should pay attention to and how they should treat staff and prisoners. The 'successful, well run and effective' prison is one, according to Wright, which: stresses care, custody and control; is safe, clean and humane; and has effective prison staff who are characterised by pride, professionalism and proficiency. Unlike DiIulio, Wright advocates reducing the paramilitary hierarchical administrative structure and increasing flexibility:

> 'The pursuit of quality requires fundamental transformation in the way most prisons operate and the way prison executives perceive their own jobs and responsibilities, their opinions about their staff, and the manner in which rewards and punishments are awarded. Initiative and responsibility must be shared throughout the organisation.'[13]

Underpinning Wright's book is a belief that good managers create good prisons. A good manager, according to Wright, has strongly held values about what staff and inmates deserve, can formulate more beliefs into visions of how their organisations should operate, and have the moral determination to see that those lofty ideas are realised.[14] The warden is expected to set the ethics and values for the establishment, stress those values in their daily actions, monitor for compliance and

12. J DiIULIO (1987) op cit, p242.
13. K WRIGHT (1994). Effective Prison Leadership, New York: William Neil Publishing, p9.
14. Ibid p143.

take appropriate corrective action.[15] Effective correctional leaders must prevent their staff becoming cynical, disenchanted and indifferent. They must constantly fight negativism and encourage an atmosphere of dignity and hope.[16] Wright identifies four things which wardens must do to achieve 'quality incarceration':

- impart respect for the rights of others among staff and inmates;
- assure fair and reasonable application of rules and regulations;
- value the lawful and reasonable relationships among people;
- provide the opportunity for personal growth in an environment without bias or hostility.[17]

The main theme to emerge from Wright's book is that wardens need to be teachers. Leadership is defined by Wright in many ways and he accepts that leadership means different things to different people. Whilst accepting that some leadership traits, such as intelligence, vitality, confidence, charisma and courage cannot be greatly influenced since they are closely tied to personality and develop across an entire span of life, Wright argues that others, such as understanding followers, ability to deal with people, motivational skills and decision making, should be taught to wardens. The Federal Bureau of Prisons has accepted the need for prison leadership and runs a leadership forum for potential wardens each year.

Wright summarises his view of prison leadership in the following way:

> 'Prison leaders can begin to make a difference in the way prisons operate by working to build a sense of community, encouraging teamwork and collaborative problem solving, and urging co-operation. The most successful leaders serve as catalysts by lifting people out of their individual self-interests and uniting them towards more lofty goals.'[18]

A valuable contribution to the literature on prison management is provided by the American Correctional Association in their 'Current Concepts in Correctional Leadership' book which contains essays from

15. Ibid p135.
16. Ibid p112.
17. Ibid p123.
18. Ibid p123.

eleven prominent leaders in corrections. In the introduction to the book James Gondles suggests that the new challenges of corrections require new skills and new abilities. He believes that these include: strong communication and supervisory skills; a clear understanding of human relationships and the ability to anticipate problems and guide staff through change. For him the challenge for the contemporary correctional leader is to have the wisdom of Solomon and the ability to manage despite an often inadequate budget, an erratic legislature and more violence-prone inmates.'[19]

Good governing in England and Wales

No equivalent volume to DiIulio's 'Governing Prisons' exists in this country. There has been no systematic study of the link between the governor's approach to governing a prison and the level of success of that prison. Good governing is not taught at the Prison Service College, as was pointed out in Chapter 2.

Academic studies tend, in general, to be written in an inaccessible style. The message may be valid and worthwhile but few governors have time to read 400 pages of text, let alone the academic grounding to challenge it critically. Governors learn their profession by word of mouth, by copying role models and by trial and error. Some governors have, however, found time to put pen to paper in an attempt to identify what they consider is the essence of good governing. One such article was written by Phil Wheatley, former governor of Hull and now Deputy Director General.[20] Wheatley believed that good governing is about a team approach, where the governor makes sure that the senior management team works together and are absolutely clear about what they are doing. The key elements of his approach to good governing are:

- setting precise and concrete standards of behaviour required of staff;
- developing a clarity of purpose and ensuring that all staff know what it is;
- encouraging and rewarding good behaviour ;
- dealing with poor performance and emphasising that slip-shod and bad work will not be tolerated;

19. AMERICAN CORRECTIONAL ASSOCIATION (1988) Current Concepts in Correctional Leadership. Lanham, MD: ACA.

20. P WHEATLEY (1992) Good governing, Prison Service Journal, Issue No 86, pp21-24.

- commanding incidents effectively by ensuring speed of decision making, clarity of communication and willingness to share the risks which staff are facing;
- providing good leadership which is consistent with the standards and purpose of the establishment;
- showing a willingness to experiment and learn from experiences;
- maintaining high visibility;
- having an understanding of inmate subcultures and a clear grasp of how a prison is kept under control and secure.

A more managerialist view of good governing was expressed by John Powls, former governor of HMP Dartmoor and now Head of Correctional Policy in the Home Office. Powls coined the term 'conviction management' to represent his view of how managers should manage. He argues that:

> 'The aspirations in the [Prison Service] purpose statement will not be achieved until a way of working which matches those gets into the guts of an organisation, to the working level. A significant element in this process is how managers manage and moreover how managers learn to manage in a new way. Such an approach represents a significant though not unwelcome culture change for Prison Service managers.'[21]

As a foundation, 'conviction management' has a set of beliefs which are central to effective management:

- management is getting things done in an organisation, economically by other people;
- all managers lead by example whether they know it or not. The example can be good, bad or indifferent;
- people believe what one does, not what one says;
- the key to effective management therefore is about what managers do which leads other people to get things done;
- the effective things that managers can do are simple, though not simplistic, behavioural skills which are more than cumulative in effect when brought together;

21. J POWLS (1991) Conviction Management, in Training and Development, October 1991, pp32-35 and November 1991, pp18-23, Institute of Training and Development.

- because they are skills they can be learned and practised, managers do not have to be a special type of person to be effective. They just have to do the right things for themselves in the right situations;
- because management is about what is done and is seen to be done, it must be performed in interpersonal situations. Nobody can be managed by remote control;
- people can spot phoneys, the flavour of the month or the latest initiative. They can also spot when managers are committed. They will react accordingly. Therefore, to be effective, managers must believe in what they are doing, that is, have conviction;
- managers will need that conviction to sustain them through self-doubt, detraction, difficulties and hard work. It also helps them to have more fun and job satisfaction because their successes mean more. Conviction helps managers to care: not in a wet or sentimental way but in a professional way about what they do and the outcome of their actions;
- no-one has all the answers. Managers should all be learning all the time and trying to improve their performance. Once they stop they become a liability. Training is therefore part of a reward for being a manager not a punishment for not performing well.

More recently, Brodie Clarke, former governor of HMP Whitemoor and now Director of Security, described his approach to good governing and how to manage change.[22] For him governors must 'know what is going on' and 'notice what is going on'. They must be aware of the health of the prison - what is working well and what is working badly. This knowledge can be obtained by collecting functional information; by collecting audit type information; taking a snapshot of an activity from time to time or by testing the various systems. In addition, governors must visit all parts of their prison to get an impression of the feel of the prison, consult staff and prisoners about their impressions and listen to external visitors. Only with this type and quality of information could governors, according to Clarke, be able to formulate a view about what problems a prison faced and where the prison must go. Once formulated the vision of the future had to be 'sold' to staff, if

22. B CLARKE (1996) The Question of Change, Prison Service Journal, Issue 106, pp30-34.

change were to take place. In order to get ownership of the changes staff should be involved in drawing up the change programme. The future then had to be described in detail to all staff. Milestones have to be set for the changes, and success at each stage demonstrated. The development of a prison had to be planned and researched, and the change programme sustained. The governor's ability to champion and drive a prison forward is critical. A number of other governors have reflected on the way their prisons are managed.[23] The theory of governing must however be translated into practice in order to produce successful prisons.

As Deputy Director General, Phil Wheatley has had the opportunity to consider what governors need to do to make prisons successful.[24] He concluded that the following were essential.

- Creation of an integrated senior management team with complementary skills and clarity about their roles.
- Clarity about the prison's long and short term direction based around strategies and plans that matched the Service's agenda and which matched available resources.
- Effective communication with staff which reflected an understanding of staff and their problems, coupled with an ability to sell a 'change' agenda and the governor's view of the direction the prison was going in.
- Decisive and effective leadership which led to the effective resolution of discipline and security problems.
- Sharp use of resources where existing practice is constantly challenged and where the prison is benchmarked against similar other prisons.
- Firm line management which set clear, demanding but achievable, objectives and then checks that they are delivered, ensuring that poor performance is addressed, at the same time as developing potential and getting the best out of staff.

23. See for example, S PRYOR (1993) The principles of population management in prisons and the application at High Down, and D WAPLINGTON (1995) The important ingredients of success at Lancaster Farm and which would work in other Young Offender Institutions, Prison Service College Library.

24. Phil Wheatley outlined his theory in a lecture to the Prison Service conference in February 2000.

Good governing in practice

One way to identify elements of successful governing is to consider a number of case studies of prisons which, at a particular point, were generally considered to be successful, well governed and effective institutions.

Many of the characteristics described in the preceding paragraphs are evident in the approach, behaviour and attitude of the governor in these case studies. The case studies have been chosen simply on the grounds that they have already been well documented by independent researchers and that the information about them is in the public domain. Senior Prison Service officials would, no doubt, be able to identify many more examples of current good practice around the Service. However, it is unfortunate that no Prison Management Journal exists in the UK, unlike in many other countries, to explore best practice in governing prisons.

(A) Holloway

Holloway in the early 1980s was well known as a 'problem prison'. The Chief Inspector of Prisons, in February 1984, deplored the lack of morale over the conflict between the operational and medical staff. A group of former Holloway prisoners established a support and campaigning group for women prisoners called 'Women in Prison'. The group protested at a succession of deaths in Holloway. As a result Holloway became a centre of media attention for a while and reports about it were published almost daily. The culmination of the protests was the creation of 'The Holloway Project Committee' announced by the Home Secretary on 12 December 1984. The Committee's Report was published in July 1985 and was welcomed by the Home Secretary, Leon Brittan, who said the report was:

> 'A valuable analysis of Holloway's difficulties. I very much welcome the Committee's positive programme for an urgent increase in the prison's remand capacity, the development of its regimes, improvements in management structure, and ways of reviewing staff deployment to ensure that the prisoners get more time in association and more access Holloway's extensive facilities.'

The project report provided a catalyst for change at Holloway with clear objectives which had received the full support of ministers and

Prison Service headquarters. A new governor was needed who would drive through the required changes. The choice in the case of Holloway was Colin Allen. Paul Rock studied the developments of Holloway between 1968 and 1988 and produced a book outlining his findings.[25] Rock's view of Colin Allen was unequivocal:

> 'Organisational change is often accomplished most effectively by new leaders, and it was just so with Colin Allen. He was what organisational theorists would call a 'transformational leader'. A charismatic man who came inevitably to personify the new order and assume an importance commensurate with the magnitude of the transition through which he had to steer the prison.'[26]

A number of key themes can be identified in Allen's approach to governing:

- ✦ consultation - a group of senior staff from across the prison were appointed to look into possible ways in which the prison might develop. All staff were asked to put forward their ideas;
- ✦ multi-group working - early discussions took place between departments to promote the idea of multi-group working and team work to break down barriers;
- ✦ openness - internal and external bodies were encouraged to inspect the inner workings of Holloway so that its original and continuing problems could not be neglected. The BBC were invited to make a documentary about Holloway in 1986;
- ✦ appointment of key staff - new members of staff were brought in to key posts including: deputy governor; principal medical officer and senior medical officer;
- ✦ movement of prison officer grades - in order to break up small groups of recalcitrant staff, male senior officers were posted to Holloway, officer grades were moved from block to block every 20 weeks and duties changed;
- ✦ managing poor performers - all members of staff were expected to make a contribution to the new Holloway. Poor

25. The majority of background information for the Holloway case study is taken from P ROCK (1996) Reconstructing a Women's Prison - the Holloway Redevelopment Project 1968 -88, Oxford: Clarendon press, to which readers should refer for a detailed comprehensive account of the changes at Holloway.

26. Op cit, p303.

performers were managed more thoroughly. Officers on sick leave were monitored more closely and one officer was dismissed in consequence;

- symbolic changes - the board of visitors were given keys and were no longer escorted around the prison. Staff were made aware that the board of visitors could inspect any area at any time. The staff car park had a fence erected around it. Many staff had had their cars damaged and the simple act of putting a fence around the car park indicated to staff that the governor cared for them and that he had done something for them as well as for prisoners;
- industrial relations - for the first few years at Holloway Allen insisted that change would be introduced gradually in consultation with the POA. However, with little movement from the POA, Allen was forced to adopt a more confrontational approach, asserting management's right to set staffing levels. The result was a strike by 235 POA members at Holloway between 30 July and 13 September 1988.

The Prison Department announced, in November 1988, that Colin Allen was to leave Holloway to join the Prison Inspectorate. Between 1985 and 1988 Holloway changed for the better. According to Stephen Tumim, then HM Chief Inspector of Prisons, in the foreword to Rock's book:

> 'a new and younger governor, Colin Allen, attempted to restore the balance. He could not restore the concept of Holloway as a secure hospital, or even as a wholly therapeutic prison such as Grendon, but he took on (without much support from his superiors in the Prison Service) the might of the local union forces and hostile pressure groups, and established a relatively civilised situation where hospital and prison existed alongside each other.'

The regime had improved dramatically: time unlocked had increased; 'free flow' had been introduced; access to the education department, swimming pool and the gymnasium had doubled and prisoners were given greater independence. A step change reduction had occurred in the number of attempted suicides, self-injuries and assaults.

(B) Lancaster Farms

The second case study is of HMYOI Lancaster Farms, under the governorship of David Waplington. Unlike Colin Allen's task of having to turn round a problem prison, David Waplington faced the challenge of opening a new institution. Lancaster Farms Young Offender Institution and Remand Centre had been built as a Category C male adult training prison to take over the role of HMP Lancaster. However, by the time David Waplington was appointed, in February 1992, population pressures in the north west of England had caused a change of policy so that HMP Lancaster remained open and Lancaster Farms became a young offender institution, holding 350 young offenders of whom two-thirds were un-sentenced remands.

A number of initial problems had to be overcome: firstly the planning for Lancaster Farms had been based on two thirds of its population being sentenced and settled. In reality it has had to operate with a maximum sentenced population of one third which had at times diminished to one sixth. Secondly, the buildings were only handed over to the governor two months prior to opening when there was still a considerable amount of construction work to be completed. Thirdly there was an increase in the population to 378 without any addition to the 150 full time employment places. These problems, coupled with being forced to receive volatile young offenders from court at too rapid a rate, could easily have led to a destabilised establishment with major control problems. However, at the time of HMCIP's inspection in November 1994 the establishment was highly commended

> 'There were many indications of a well-run, safe and constructive establishment. It was very clean with no sign of graffiti; cells were the tidiest and cleanest we have seen; evening association was more like a first class, well-organised boys' club than a remand centre. Every adolescent had an opportunity to attend education, training or work which was relevant.'[27]

The Chief Inspector had a clear view of the reasons for such a positive establishment:

27. Report by HM Chief Inspector of Prisons on HMYOI and RC Lancaster Farms (1995), London.

'We found strong leadership from the governor and his senior management team and this, in turn, gave staff confidence in their own abilities and allowed them to develop initiatives. The establishment's Statement of Purpose - 'Our aim is to prevent the next victim' - was typical of the positive message going out to both staff and inmates. Lancaster Farms is well on the way to achieving its model establishment aim.'[28]

The strong leadership described by HMCIP was based on the governor:

- working long hours and maintaining high levels of visibility around the establishment;
- communicating directly and openly with all staff and inmates;
- creating an atmosphere in which staff felt confident in putting forward ideas, creating initiatives and managing inmates;
- involving everyone in a multi-disciplinary approach and encouraging co-operation between departments;
- rewarding good work openly and only giving constructive criticism;
- creating an effective communications system in which he (or his deputy) met representatives from all areas at a team briefing each day, which was then relayed to individual teams the following day;
- routinely attending meetings chaired by his managers;
- talking to all new members of staff during their one week induction in order to describe his personal vision for and ethos of the establishment;
- working with the Trust for Adolescence to create specific training for staff working with young people in custody;
- setting clear standards of behaviour for inmates, reflected in a comprehensive anti-bullying strategy, resulting in a controlled and safe environment; and
- creating a system of rewards and sanctions which gave a clear structure to inmates with histories of non-conforming behaviour.

28. HM Chief Inspector of Prisons Judge Stephen Tumin quoted in a press release at the time of the publication of the report on HMYOI Lancaster Farms, 7 July 1995.

The success of Lancaster Farms was also recently acknowledged by the Prison Reform Trust which described it as an institution which was 'successfully delivering the balance of security, control and justice which Lord Woolf said was the core of good prison management'.[29] Their report goes on to state:

> 'Lancaster Farms has been the recipient of many accolades since its opening in 1993. The praise emanated from a wide variety of sources, from the Prison Inspectorate, academic bodies, journalists and pressure groups. The impressive record includes a National Security Audit Team 'Superior' rating, a Prison Service Internal Audit 'Good' rating. The prison has had only one escape since opening, and no completed suicides. Assault levels and staff absence are low. In a climate of cutbacks the prison maintains a high level of purposeful out-of-cell activity. The Prison Reform Trust was greatly impressed by Lancaster Farms. There is a distinct vision and clarity of purpose. Staff are well trained and enthusiastic. The prison regime is innovative, providing a high level of activity and regular contact with community groups. The education department has achieved tremendous success with a very volatile, fast moving population. Special initiatives such as the anti-bullying and 'coping in custody' courses tackle some of the key issues faced by a Young Offenders Institution.'

The part played by the governor in achieving success was clear to the report's author: '[the governor's] vision and enthusiasm have played a central role in the establishment's success'.

(C) Brixton

In the early 1990s Brixton typified all that could go wrong in a prison. HMCIP, in a report published in 1990, described the prison as 'a corrupting and depressing institution'.[30] In 1991, the European Committee for the Prevention of Torture found that the 'pernicious combination of overcrowding, inadequate regime activities, lack of integral sanitation and poor hygiene' in Brixton and in some other

29. C SPARKS (19970) Achieving Prisons - Lancaster Farms : Preventing the next victim. London: Prison Reform Trust.

30. Report of an Inspection of HMP Brixton (1990) London: HMSO.

English prisons amounted to 'inhuman and degrading treatment'[31] A vivid description of the problems facing Brixton was provided by Derek Lewis:

> 'It regularly held up to 1,150 prisoners, over 50 per cent more than its normal capacity. The majority still slopped out, the wings were pervaded by the stench of excreta emanating from the cells and from the recesses on the landings where prisoners emptied their pots in the mornings. The cells and wings were dark and decaying, daubed in depressing shades of brown and green so admired by the nineteenth century prison-builders, with much of the paint flaking and peeling. Any attempts at cleaning were at best half-hearted. The notorious 'Fraggle Rock' (F wing) was like bedlam: mentally ill prisoners were held together, and the barren building echoed to their cries and the drumming of fists on doors ... many prisoners spent all but an hour a day locked in their cells, while for those who did come out there was little to do.'[32]

The security of the prison was dramatically breached in July 1991 when two alleged IRA terrorists Nessan Quinlivan and Pearse McCauley shot their way out. As a result the governor was told to take immediate pre-retirement leave and Dr. Andrew Coyle, a governor from the Scottish Prison Service, was asked to take command. The new governor was instructed to prevent further escapes and to improve Brixton's performance dramatically. This was a far from simple task given Brixton's history and endemic resistance to change. However, something had to be done quickly to improve security and to end Brixton's record of 14 suicides between 1989 and 1990. Coyle recognised the daunting task ahead:

> 'There is a particular challenge in taking over an organisation which has been rocked to its foundations. If it has reached its nadir there is a great opportunity, particularly if it has an

31. Council of Europe (1991) Report to the United Kingdom Government on the visit to the UK carried out by the European Committee for the Prevention of Torture and Inhuman and Degrading Treatment or Punishment, Council of Europe, Strasbourg.

32. D LEWIS (1997) Hidden Agenda: Politics, Law and Disorder, London: Hamish Hamilton, p43.

> innate strength and confidence, to rebuild it within a new and more dynamic context'.[33]

The approach taken by Coyle to bring about the needed change was to let the public, through the media, have a glimpse of what life inside was like. The press coverage brought a better understanding of the problems which faced Brixton and much needed resources and a commitment from outside agencies to help. Various initiatives at Brixton led to mentally disordered men being transferred to hospital. Coyle closed the infamous F wing and distributed the remaining disturbed prisoners to one of five health care wards where they received proper medical attention. Potentially suicidal prisoners were no longer isolated in cells without any personal comfort or possessions but were held in small wards where they could mix with other prisoners and where staff had time to listen to them. Visiting facilities were improved and external organisations encouraged to send representatives into the prison on a regular basis to help prisoners prepare for release.

Coyle recognised the need to look forward and to get the staff to focus on improvement to achieve success. The time had come for Brixton under leadership of its governor to take charge of its destiny . The means Coyle used to do this was a strategic planning exercise entitled 'Brixton 2000'. The document made clear to staff that:

> 'We have a unique opportunity to plan for the future in a way which will enable Brixton to develop its full potential as a local prison, which will create an environment which is just and safe for all who live and work here, which will provide prisoners with the opportunities for personal development and which will encourage staff to make full use of their initiative and talents.'[34]

The broad parameters of the plan were drawn up by the senior management team. All staff were encouraged to study it, to consider how it affected their area of work and to offer suggestions as to how the plan could be amended and improved. Following the period of

33. A COYLE (1994) The Prisons we Deserve, London: Harper Collins, p116. A detailed discussion of the changes at Brixton can be found in Chapter 8.

34. HM Prison Service (1992) Brixton 2000: A strategic management plan to take Brixton Prison towards the year 2000.

consultation a strategic plan emerged to which everyone had been able to contribute and of which everyone could claim ownership.

The strategic plan produced by Coyle and his senior team was informed by a vision and a set of shared values to which all staff were asked to subscribe: They included:

- the provision of appropriate custody in safe and decent conditions;
- openness, fairness and justice;
- the need to establish high quality standards;
- the high commitment of Brixton staff and management's commitment to staff;
- trained staff providing programmes which offer prisoners opportunities and dignity;
  sharing and supporting difficult tasks by using the team approach; providing opportunities for staff and prisoners; and
- positive relationships between staff and prisoners.[35]

The plan made quite clear that a wide range of issues would have to be dealt with if Brixton 2000 was to become a reality. These elements were reduced to seven strategic issues on which the staff were encouraged to focus:

- transforming Brixton into a community prison;
- redeveloping the Brixton estate;
- developing a team approach;
- managing for change;
- establishing a new style of working for all staff;
- setting up a 'quality initiative' and;
- promoting Brixton Prison.

HMCIP inspected Brixton in January 1996 to monitor its progress. Sir David Ramsbotham commented that:

35. Ibid p2.

> 'Brixton Prison in London has improved significantly in the last three years and is now a well managed, well ordered and more caring establishment.'[36]

Lewis was similar in his praise of what can be achieved by a governor with vision and leadership:

> 'Brixton had been transformed. Overcrowding and slopping out had gone, the buildings had been refurbished and cleaned up. F wing had been converted for use by normal prisoners and renamed G wing and the previous occupants of F wing re-housed in a clean, light and humane health care centre. Prisoners were out of their cells and more active. It was a case study of what can be done by those who take charge of the future and approach it with optimism, rather than being managed by events.'[37]

(D) Garth

When Bill Rose-Quirie took over the governorship at Garth in 1992, he became the prison's third governor since it had opened in 1988. The prison had a very poor reputation and had many problems. One landing had even been converted to take the segregation unit overspill. Yet within six years the prison had received a 'good' security audit rating, a 'superior' standards audit rating, had been called 'an example of a very well run prison' by HM Inspector of Prisons, had achieved the Investors in People award, received a government 'charter mark' for excellence and the governor himself had been awarded the 1998 Office of Public Management Leadership Award.

The 1997 Inspection report on Garth makes clear what had been achieved in a short time:

> 'If we were in the habit of doing so we would recommend HMP Garth as a prison of good practice, by which I mean that it should be held up to the Prison Service as an example of an extremely well run prison, where difficult prisoners, during the most difficult part of what are, in many cases, long

36. HM Chief Inspector of Prisons (1996) Press release at the time of the publication of a full inspection of HMP Brixton, Home Office, London.

37. LEWIS op cit p44.

sentences, are challenged and not allowed to sit back and idle their time through, in which there are many good practices that could be followed, with advantage, by others. There is an impressive sense of purpose in whatever part of the prison one visits, exemplified by quite the best staff training programme that we have seen anywhere, master-minded by a dedicated and capable Principal Officer. If confirmation were needed of the importance of getting staff training right, as basis for a well run prison, it is amply provided at Garth. The Governor governs through a team of managers, but what impressed all members of the Inspectorate, who took part in the inspection, was that each member of the team was not only on top of his or her job, but knew how it related to the overall prison strategy. It was a real pleasure to discuss not only current arrangements but also future possibilities with a group of people who clearly had thought, and were thinking, about such matters as a matter of course.

We were impressed by the quality achieved, the determination of staff to achieve a high standard and the sensible provision of services to prisoners. Overall, Garth should be seen as a centre of excellence in the work staff undertake with long-term prisoners. The policies adopted at Garth ensured a balance between maintaining order and allowing each individual the opportunity to come to terms with his time in prison before release becomes a reality. Garth also ensured that prisoners were continually confronted with their behaviour, attitudes and reasons for offending. It is a duty which the public rightly expect of the Prison Service.

The governor, managers and staff are to be congratulated on the standards they had achieved in providing a balanced and purposeful regime. Good order was maintained through simple rules which were enforced by a sensible and strong relationship between staff and prisoners. the atmosphere which pervaded the prison was one of control and a sense of direction.'

The change brought about at Garth had much to do with the approach and ability of the governor. He quickly created a climate for change, empowered staff and developed a vision of where the prison was going and what he wanted it to be like. Specific requirements were set:

- customer focus;
- quality standards;
- a functional business plan and budgets; and
- internal audits and local key performance indicators.

There was much delegation and staff were empowered to deliver. Self managed teams were created which were small autonomous work groups which helped to flatten management structures, promoted team work and empowered staff at all levels. Attention was paid to succession planning and high profile training. Each member of staff was given a development handbook and drew up individual training logs linked to job competency profiles. Successes were celebrated and staff rewarded. Attempts were made to develop a learning organisation, which avoided a blame culture. Professional staff were valued and respected. Other staff were encouraged to leave. The governor maintained a high profile and ensured that everyone knew where the prison was going.

POSTSCRIPT

Governing prisons is difficult. Governing prisons well must rank amongst the most complex, challenging and arduous of all occupations. Governors are expected to be effective general managers who can plan, resource, organise, direct, communicate with and motivate their staff. Yet this must be done within a custodial setting. Prisons are *sui generis* and require additional skills, abilities and knowledge. Governors must achieve a balance between security, care and justice. They must be able to switch to command mode at short notice and deal with major incidents such as fire, escape and violent disorder. Governors must demonstrate leadership and commitment to the staff and prisoners. They must discipline staff, where appropriate, using the code of conduct and discipline, and also act in a quasi-judicial role when adjudicating on prisoner misbehaviour. Governors must ensure that justice exists and is perceived to exist. All this must be done in the complex, intensive, coercive and highly charged environment of a prison. The job is made even more challenging because everything must be done under the watchful eye of Parliament, HMCIP, pressure groups, prisoners' families and line management. In short: 'A governor must be simultaneously a manager, leader, co-ordinator, expert and administrator.'[1]

Each of these roles requires specific activities:

- manager - monitoring and assessing the processes which implement service policy, making things happen, defining tasks and making decisions;
- leader - offering a style of behaviour appropriate to the establishment and its tasks;
- co-ordinator - seeing that the complexity of activities initiated by Headquarters at policy level are relayed synergistically at local level;
- expert - using past experience in making decisions; and
- administrator - knowing the policy, its implications and seeing that it is carried out at all levels in the establishment.

Governors have a dual role. They are the representatives of Headquarters and the broader Prison Service in their prison. As such they must interpret and implement policy and maintain corporate

1. B REED (1985) Exercising authority as a governor in the Prison Service, Grubb Institute.

responsibility. Yet they are also the head of the establishment and in this role they must represent the operational view to Headquarters, all the while effectively governing their establishment and meeting the expectations of both staff and prisoners.

The essence of the job has remained the same over decades. However, if anything, the role of the prison governor is becoming more complex with increased demands being made on them. Devolution of prisoner casework, financial responsibility and personnel matters to governors has increased flexibility but also increased complexity. This, together with the increased external pressure from the courts, ombudsmen and MPs have made governors more visible, accountable and exposed to challenge and criticism. This book is intended to raise awareness about some of the key issues of governing. If it contributes to making the work of governing prisons more comprehensible, and improves, in some small way, the ability of governors to govern then it has been worthwhile.

For the wider audience, it is hoped that this book challenges some of the stereotypes, described in the introductory chapter, by highlighting the complexity involved in governing prisons. We hope that we have shown that being an effective governor requires more than just being an able manager or skilled administrator.

It is appropriate to end this book with some words from the Woolf Report which encapsulate the importance of prison governors and their staff:

> 'The quality of our prisons in the future will primarily depend on the energy and ability of all those involved, in whatever capacity, in running our prisons.'[2]

2. Prison Disturbances April 1990 (Woolf Report) (1991) Cmnd 1456, London: HMSO, para 2.59.

APPENDIX 1

ROLE AND TASK OF THE PRISON SERVICE

Aim

The Prison Service is a part of the criminal justice system which works to two overarching aims:

- ✦ to reduce crime and the fear of crime, and their social and economic costs;
- ✦ to dispense justice fairly and efficiently and to promote confidence in the rule of law.

These aims and their associated targets are set out in the Public Service Agreement for the criminal justice system.

Objectives

Deriving from these overarching aims, the Prison Service works within the Home Office Public Service Agreement:

- ✦ to protect the public by holding in custody those committed by the courts in a safe, decent, and healthy environment;
- ✦ to reduce crime by providing constructive regimes which address offending behaviour, improve educational and work skills and promote law-abiding behaviour in custody and after release.

Principles

In support of the specified aim and objectives is a statement of the ways in which the Prison Service works towards them and the conduct expected from staff.

In undertaking our work, all members of the Prison Service will:

- ✦ deal fairly, openly, and humanely with prisoners and all others who come into contact with us;
- ✦ encourage prisoners to address offending behaviour and respect others;
- ✦ value and support each other's contribution;
- ✦ promote equality of opportunity for all and combat discrimination wherever it occurs;

- work constructively with criminal justice agencies and other organisations;
- obtain best value from resources available.

APPENDIX 2

PRISON SERVICE

CORE COMPETENCE FRAMEWORK

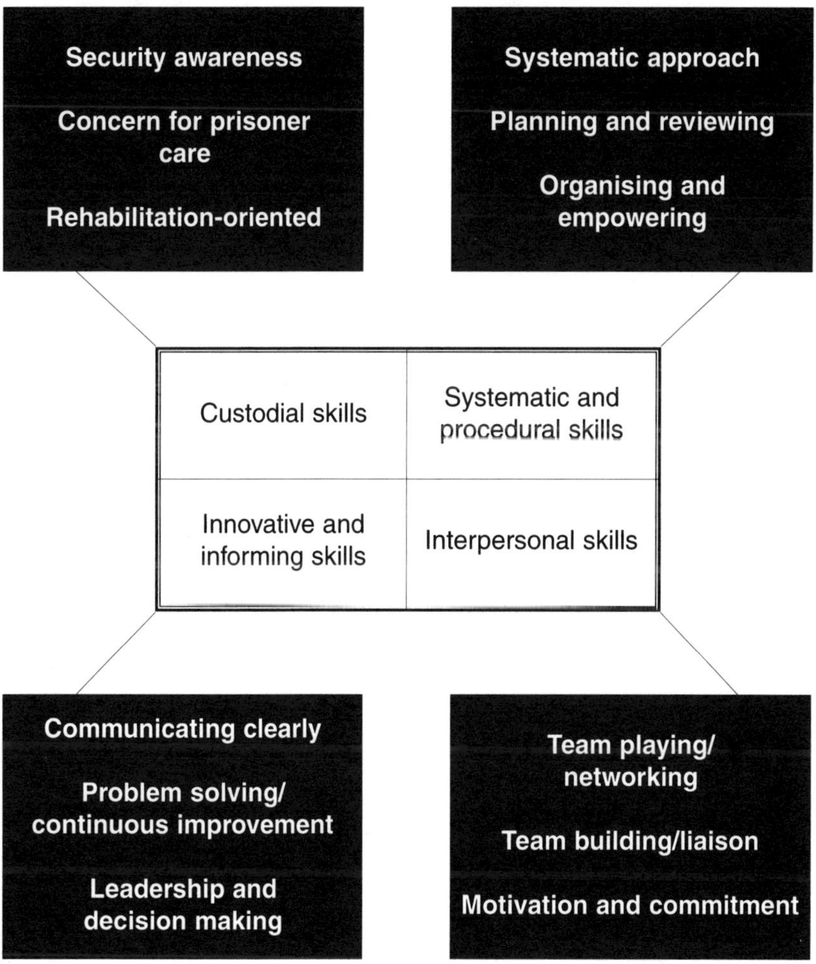

APPENDIX 3

CITIZEN'S CHARTER : STANDARDS OF SERVICE

The Prison Service is committed to the principles of public service in the Citizen's Charter. This statement, together with our Statement of Purpose, Vision, Goals and Values, explains how we act on these principles in meeting our responsibilities:

- to the public;
- to prisoners;.
- to their families, friends, legal representatives and other visitors to prisons.

The Public

We are committed to delivering our services with maximum efficiency to provide the best possible value for money:

- we will keep prisoners in custody;
- we will work with prisoners to address their offending behaviour and help them prepare for their successful return to the community;
- we will co-operate closely with other criminal justice agencies, such as the police and probation services, to contribute to the effectiveness of the wider criminal justice system;
- our key targets and performance against those targets will be published every year in our Business Plan and Annual Report.

Prisoners

- you will be given a general information pack when you are first admitted to prison including details about visiting arrangements, sending letters, and how to complain;
- you will also be given detailed information about the facilities and services at your own establishment;
- your preferences will be taken into account wherever possible in deciding what work you will do and what education or training you will receive;
- we are setting up regular prisoner surveys in all establishments to find out what you think about regimes, conditions and other aspects of prison life;

- you will be treated fairly and given reasons for decisions: these will be given in writing if you make a formal complaint;
- if you have a complaint, you can take it up with a member of staff, ask to see the governor, use the written requests and complaints procedures or raise it with a member of the independent board of visitors. (More details are given in the leaflet 'How to Make a Request or Complaint');
- A Prisons Ombudsman will be appointed later in 1993 to review complaints which are not satisfactorily settled by the requests and complaints system.

Visitors to prison

Our aim is to ensure that visitors to prisons, including prisoners' families, friends and legal representatives, are treated courteously and professionally at all times:

- we will try to provide decent facilities for visitors, convenient visiting times, helpful information and a reasonable amount of privacy at all our establishments;
- staff who come into contact with prisoners and the public will normally wear name badges.

Developing our standards of service

We are preparing a Code of Standards in consultation with interested groups, including prisoners. We plan to publish the Code by the end of 1993. It will set detailed standards for the full range of services we provide, including accommodation, activities, health care and visiting arrangements.

We will review the present statement when the Code is published.

Prisoner 'compacts' are also being used on a trial basis in a number of prisons. These tell prisoners about the facilities, opportunities and choice available to them in prison and what is expected of them in return. If successful, they will be introduced in other prisons.

We shall consider how best to develop local statements of service standards in a way which is consistent with these initiatives.

HM Inspectorate of Prisons

HM Chief Inspector of Prisons (HMCIP) has a statutory duty to inspect prisons and report to the Home Secretary on a wide range of issues including the treatment of prisoners, conditions in prison and value for money. HMCIP is wholly independent of the Prison Service and his reports are published.

Further information

The Prison Service's first Corporate and Business Plans, published on 1 April 1993, set out detailed strategies for 1993 to 1996 and specific targets set by the Home Secretary for 1993-94. These Plans are available in prison libraries.

More information about the work of the Prison Service, and our performance against these targets, will be given in our Annual Report.

Prison Service, April 1993

APPENDIX 4

PERFORMANCE AGAINST KEY PERFORMANCE INDICATORS 1992-98

KPI 1: Escapes

The number of Category A escapes. The number of escapes from prisons and escorts, expressed as a proportion of the average population (excluding prisoners recaptured within 15 minutes, where no further criminal offence has been committed).

Table A.1: Category A Escapes 1992-98

Year	Category A Escapes
1992-93	2
1993-94	0
1994-95	8
1995-96	3
1996-97	0
1997-98	0

Table A.2: Escapes from prisons and from escorts 1992 -1998

	Assaults on prisoners	Rate of assaults on prisoners %	Assaults on staff and others	Rate of assaults on staff and others %	Total assaults	Total assault rate %
1992-93	2,062	4.7	2,413	5.5	4,475	10.2
1993-94	2,448	5.3	3,207	7.0	5,655	12.3
1994-95	2,438	4.9	3,301	6.7	5,739	11.6
1995-96	2,607	5.1	2,873	5.6	5,480	10.6
1996-97	2,748	4.8	2,528	4.5	5,276	9.3
1997-98	3,005	4.8	2,528	4.6	5,861	9.0

KPI 3: Drug misuse

The rate of positive results of random tests.

1997-98 20.8%

KPI 4: Overcrowding

The number of prisoners held in units of accommodation intended for fewer numbers.

	Prisoners held three to a cell designed for one	Prisoners held two to a cell designed for one	Prisoners held in police cells
1992-93	468	7,251	715
1993-94	82	7,771	67
1994-95	0	8,427	163
1995-96	0	8,505	30
1996-97	0	9,494	0
1997-98	0	11,548	0

KPI 5: Purposeful Activity

The number of hours which, on average prisoners spend in purposeful activity

	Weekly average hours of purposeful activity per prisoner
1992-93	23.7
1993-94	24.7
1994-95	26.2
1995-96	25.2
1996-97	23.8
1997-98	23.3

KPI 6: Time unlocked

The proportion of prisoners held in establishments which normally unlock all prisoners on the standard or enhanced regime for at least ten hours per weekday.

	Percentage of population held in prisons which unlock of 12+ hours per weekday %	Percentage of population held in prisons which unlock all prisoners on the standard and enhanced regimes for 10+ hours per weekday %
1992-93	24.0	-
1993-94	29.0	-
1994-95	40.0	-
1995-96	37.5	-
1996-97	-	65.0
1997-98	-	62.0

KPI 7: Offending behaviour programmes

The number of completions by prisoners of programmes accredited as effective in reducing re-offending.

	No. of completions by prisoners of Sex Offender Treatment Programmes	Total No. of completions by prisoners of accredited programmes
1996-97	663	1,373
1997-98	671	2,240

KPI 8: Cost per prison place

The average cost per prison place (current expenditure per baseline Certified Normal Accommodation).

	1992-1993	1993-1994	1994-1995	1995-1996	1996-1997	1997-1998
Current total expenditure (£m)	1,179.3	1,233.7	1,263.6	1,328.8	1,372.2	1,460.9
Average Baseline CNA	51,900	53,020	54,022	54,959	56,538	63,500
Cost per place (£ cash terms)	22,723	23,080	23,391	24,178	24,271	23,940
Cost per place (1992-1993 prices)	22,123	22,427	22,391	22,525	21,973	21,144

KPI 9: Staff training

Average number of days staff spend in training.

1997-97	5.4
1996-98	7.8

APPENDIX 5

ALPHABETICAL INDEX OF ALL PRISON SERVICE STANDARDS

Accommodation
Business planning
Cash
Categorisation and allocation
Catering
Cell furniture and equipment
Communication (prisoner)
Conduct and discipline (staff)
Contingency planning/incidents
Death in custody
Disabled prisoners
Discharge
Discipline (prisoners)
Disclosure of information
Dogs
Drug policy
Education (inc. pysical education)
Enterprises
Equal opportunities (staff)
Escorts
Expenses
Family life (establishment and maintenance)
Filling vacancies by internal means
Finance
Fire safety
Grievance procedure
Health services for prisoners
Home detention curfew (HDC)
Human resource planning
Hygiene
Incentives and earned privileges
Induction programme
Industrial relations
Internal communications
IT strategy
Legal aid and bail
Life sentence
Maintenance of all PS buildings
Management
Mother and baby units
Occupational safety and health
Offending behaviour
Palliative care
Parole
Performance management
Physical security
Prison Service instructions system
Prison shop
Prisoner information system
Procurement
Property
Race relations (prisoners)
Reception
Recruitment
Regimes
Religion
Requests and complaints systems
Safer prisons (anti-bullying)
Security intelligence
Security procedures
Segregation units
Sentence calculation
Sentence management and planning
Sickness absence and unsatisfactory attendance
Staff care and welfare
Standards for compliance
Suicide and self-harm reduction
Temporary release
Throughcare and resettlement
Training
Transfer of prisoners
Treatment of the public and criminal justice agencies
Use of force
Video links
Visits